LIBRARY SCHOOL CLOSINGS: four case studies

by
MARION PARIS

The Scarecrow Press, Inc.
Metuchen, N.J., & London
1988

378.1553
P217l
1988

Library of Congress Cataloging-in Publication Data

Paris, Marion, 1948-
    Library school closings : four case studies / by Marion Paris
        p.   cm.
    Bibliography : p.
    Includes index.
    ISBN 0-8108-2130-3
    1. Library school closings--United States--Case studies.
2. Library schools--United States--Administration--Case studies.
3. Library education--United States--Case studies.   I. Title.
Z668.P37 1988   88-7276

To library education--past, present, and future

Catherine Sciascia, Laurie Hermance-Moore, and Gordon S. Banholzer, Jr. have my thanks for the word processing and indexing skills they acquired at the University of Alabama's Graduate School of Library Service.

TABLE OF CONTENTS

CHAPTER 1

INTRODUCTION

In 1978 the Graduate School of Librarianship at the University of Oregon closed its doors as a result, according to the university's president William Boyd, of financial problems due to declining enrollments, a "substantial pool" of unemployed and underemployed librarians in the state, and the failure to develop a strong curriculum and faculty.[1]

What may have caused at best only mild concern in the library education community at the time--the closing of a library school--has some nine years later assumed crisis proportions, as eleven additional schools have either closed or announced plans to do so. According to Dyer and O'Connor, officials of many of the library schools in this country fear a domino effect; that is, that the twelve closings will somehow bring about the demise of even more library schools.[2]

Yet, as Stueart has observed,

> Librarianship, one of the premier
> professions in the communication
> and information fields, stands at the
> entrance to a gateway of opportunity
> that few professions have ever ex-
> perienced and which will probably
> never come this way again.[3]

In response to technological changes that took place during the 1970s, many graduate schools of library science have been renamed schools of library and information science. Their curricula have been augmented to embrace such nontraditional courses and specializations as information management, information brokerage or entrepreneur-

ship, telecommunications, records management, and office
automation; in addition to providing timely instruction in
information storage and retrieval, computer programming,
automated indexing and abstracting, and library automation. Moreover, Galvin, acknowledging the growing economic importance of information in his introduction to
Debons and King's *The Information Professional: Survey
of an Emerging Field*, suggests that the missions of schools
of librarianship be further broadened to meet society's
burgeoning information needs.[4] Griffiths maintains that
the role of the information intermediary will survive and
indeed grow as a result of proliferating online information
systems. New functions--database searcher, trainer, and
information adviser, for example--have emerged.[5] It is a
matter of considerable interest and speculation, then, as to
why, given at least the potential for enlarging their frames
of reference, twelve library schools have ceased operation
in less than a decade.

The total number of M.L.S. graduates, as tabulated
by the Association for Library and Information Science
Education (ALISE) from data submitted by member and
nonmember library schools decreased to 3,820 in 1984, a
32 percent decline from the 5,029 M.L.S. recipients
counted in 1978, the first year such statistics were made
available by the then Association of American Library
Schools (AALS).[6,7] Library and library-related job possi-
bilities for holders of the Master of Library Science have
begun to recover from a low experienced in the late 1970s;
and while entry level compensation has risen over the past
several years, incidence of starting salaries in the low teens
is still not rare.[8]

It is suspected, however, that despite the grave implications which declining enrollments, a soft job market,
and dwindling numbers of applicants have for the future
viability of library schools, other factors as well may
obtain. Dyer and O'Connor suggest that some of those include such conditions as "poor morale, inability to secure

outside funding, and declining university support."[9] The
third condition, declining university support, would appear
to have two dimensions: quantitative, affecting salaries,
equipment, facilities, and student financial aid; and
qualitative, reflected in university administrators' attitudes
toward and expectations of the library school. Finally, it
has been implied in the general literature that competition
from a nearby institution cannot be overlooked chiefly in,
but not limited to, situations where the predator program is
public and its prey, private.[10]

It is possible that some or perhaps all of the conditions named above have variously affected the viability
of American M.L.S. programs accredited by the Committee
on Accreditation (COA) of the American Library Association. To what extent individual programs have been in-
fluenced by specific conditions and, more important, what
common conditions the now defunct programs may have
shared, has not been studied. Aside from those discussed
in the private musings of library educators, however,
variables that might either be related to the closings or, if
present, suggest that a program might be in jeopardy, remain obscure. It is the purpose of the present study, then,
to identify conditions relating to library school closings
that have occurred in the United States since 1978.

THEORETICAL CONTEXT

Retrenchment in Higher Education

Retrenchment--college and university response to
institutional decline resulting from dwindling enrollments
in, and financial support of, higher education--poses the
often agonizing question of how institutions confronting
such decline can plan and respond in ways that will be
consonant with their basic educational goals.[11] Awareness
of the need for retrenchment grew during the past decade

as some 29 percent of all postsecondary institutions saw
declining enrollment from 1970 to 1978.[12] Financial support, subject to economic fluctuations caused by the 1974-
75 recession and recovery, the 1978-79 downturn, and
numerous tax-cutting plans initiated by state governments,
could no longer be counted on. Frequently a spiral of decline set in, where in a typical scenario fewer new students
led to cuts in expenditures; those led to reductions in personnel, services, and maintenance; those in turn led to
increased intraorganizational conflict, a precursor of low-
ered faculty and student morale. In some institutions such
conditions led, ultimately, to closing.[13]

    Patterns of resistance to decline emerged first.
Well-documented, they include moves to recruit older or
so-called non-traditional students or those from previously
untapped geographic areas; the addition of more vocation-
ally-oriented courses to the curriculum; the offering of
more off-campus or evening programs; the lowering of
admissions standards; and the searching out of new sources
of revenue, typically from private sources. Institutions
perfected the art of resistance to decline in the form of the
above strategies and others during the 1970s.[14]

    It soon became clear, however, that while those
strategies could be employed somewhat successfully over
the short term, something else would be necessary for
longterm survival: that something was adaptation, or
reconciliation of institutional goals to new circumstances.
As Mingle and Norris are careful to point out,

> It [adaptation] does not mean resig-
> nation. Adapting successfully calls
> for more than mere cutting of ex-
> penditures in the face of revenue
> shortfall; it also calls for careful
> planing in anticipation of de-
> cline....[15]

A widely accepted means to organizational well-being is planning, defined by McClure as

> the process of identifying organizational goals and objectives, developing programs or services to accomplish those objectives, and evaluating the success of those programs compared to the stated objectives.[16]

Yet, planning tools have negligible influence in many retrenchment situations.[17] As explained by Clark, traditional planning systems rely heavily on the notion of rational decision making, as well as on the idea that educational organizations are goal-based entities. Recent organization theory suggests, however, that educational organizations are at best loosely-coupled systems, characterized by departmental units acting independently and often in conflict of one another; obscure continuity, if any, in educational planning; and disconnected communication across hierarchical levels.[18] In short, Clark has written, "the requisite conditions for institution-wide goal-based planning are seldom found in educational organizations."[19]

An alternative to traditional planning known as reassessment, a combination of internal reallocation of resources and/or contraction of size and scope, has been put to use with more success at some universities.[20] Although reallocation has long been utilized as part of the institutional budgeting process--commonly as a tool wielded by budget officials--its use in joint administration-faculty reassessment programs is new. In such joint involvement inherent difficulties exist, most notably with those persons who are uncomfortable accepting the premise that new or expanded programs often come at the expense of old ones.

Vanderbilt University, faced in 1979 with conflict brought about by various needs for retrenchment decisions,

formed two parallel reassessment panels, one composed of
faculty and one of administrators, which developed seven
criteria to be used in evaluating the institution's academic
programs. Those criteria, because of their comprehensive-
ness-- presented here for illustrative purposes, include the
following:

1. <u>Essentiality of the Program to a University</u>
(required/not required.) How central is this program to the
"generic" ideal of the university? How essential to this
particular institution?

2. <u>Quality of the Program</u>
(excellent/strong/adequate/weak). An excellent program is
one with a potential quality matched by few institutions.

3. <u>Need for the Program</u> (high/medium/low).
Intended to be normative, calling for the university's "own
view of society's educational needs without regard for
whether the members of society see them in exactly the
same way."

4. <u>Demand for the Program</u> (high/medium/low).
Demand for the program is measured in three ways: by
enrollment of majors, by enrollment of other students, and
by demand for the program's majors in the employment
market.

5. <u>Locational Advantage</u> (yes/no). Are there clearly
demonstrable advantages of the program's specific location
at Vanderbilt? Geographic advantages? Demographic?
Cultural? Other?

6. <u>Cost-Revenue Relationships</u>
(favorable/unfavorable.) Data on student/faculty ratios,
cost per credit hour, prospects for external funding, and
other measures are used to assess the program's status as a
financial asset or liability.

7. Cost Implications of Maintaining or Changing
Program Role (high/medium/low). How much are the increases (or decreases) in cost required to bring the program
to a desired level of fulfillment?[21]

A notable strength of that approach for Vanderbilt
was that it enabled participants to assemble a composite
picture and thus to establish priorities, since university
officials believed that program judgments did not, and
should not, depend upon a single factor. Vanderbilt's first
round of reassessment reallocated $1.5 million from admin-
istrative services and athletic tuition subsidies to improve-
ments in faculty salaries and additional funding for the
library. Also recommended was that several academic programs be studied in a second round with a view toward
future contraction, but for some, expansion.[22] At Vanderbilt reassessment met with success. Such an ostensibly
reasoned approach, officials maintained, would prevent
hasty or illadvised cuts that have been effected at institutions where administrators bowed to pressure to "do
something."

Implications for Library School Closings

Only two papers, that by Dyer and O'Connor cited
above and an additional 1983 *Library Journal* piece by
Eshelman, directly speculate on factors possibly related to
the spate of library school closings.[23] Broadly speaking,
the research literature in higher education is also of limited
assistance in generalizing about related factors as much of
what has been published exists in case form. Moreover,
recent studies which have been undertaken analyze closings
of whole colleges or universities, while the present investigation sought to examine the closing of only one academic unit or division of an educational institution. This
is not to say, however, that clues cannot be found.

Miles and Huberman have written that a conceptual
framework "explains, either graphically or in narrative

form, the main dimensions to be studied, the key factors, or variables, and the presumed relationships among them....They can be rudimentary or elaborate, theory driven or common sensical, descriptive or causal."[24] It has been demonstrated that within the academic community, evaluation and review figure prominently in retrenchment decisions precipitated to a great extent by institutional financial decline. It is not a purpose of the present study literally to evaluate defunct Master of Library Science programs emulating the efforts of a panel like Vanderbilt's. Rather, the Vanderbilt reassessment model has been employed theoretically to serve a twofold purpose: first as a logical structure in which to place factors only conjectured to be related to library school closings, and second as a basis for question (i.e., hypothesis) formulation and subsequent case analysis.

Theoretical Application of the Vanderbilt Model

        As described above, the model encompasses seven criteria. Those may be used to contain much of what has been written about library school closings.

        Essentiality, or relevance to the university's mission, may rest on qualitative judgments made by persons in possession of a limited understanding of the library school's own mission and goals. Hyatt *et al.* have written that "largest reductions normally are made in academic programs not central to main instructional and/or research purposes of the institution."[25] Studying defunct special libraries, Matarazzo found that continuing justification to management of the library's existence was instrumental to survival, since decisions to terminate library service were made at the highest corporate level by individuals unsympathetic to the library.[26] Parallels can be drawn with library schools: presumably it is possible and desirable for library school administrators regularly to keep their superiors apprised of their schools' essentiality to the university's larger purpose, for as White has noted, "schools seeking to avoid the ax have quite correctly attempted to marshal their own forces."[27]

Quality pertains not so much to intra-institutional rankings where disparate departments or schools are pitted against one another as it does to extra-institutional potential for excellence as measured, for example, against other library schools. As White has written,

> The question of quality is not really defined for library education on the campus except in terms of demonstrable perceptions. Most library school administrators and faculty would just as soon keep it that way. We prefer to evaluate ourselves and not be judged by others whose appreciation of what we do we distrust.[28]

For library education programs the best known and most widely, although by no means universally, accepted index of quality is the approval of a site visit team dispatched to each school every seven years by the Committee on Accreditation (COA) of the American Library Association. COA accrediting decisions, however, may merely be an assurance of acceptable quality. Library school closings may be precipitated less frequently by action of accrediting bodies than by unrelated decisions at individual universities.[29] There may be little, if any, relationship between the quality of a program as determined by an accreditation visit and its eventual demise, although conditional accreditation or complete loss of it has apparently occurred prior to several of the closings.[30,31]

Need is a "normative judgment based on 'the university's own view of society's educational needs without

regard for whether the members of society see them in
exactly the same way.'"[32] Indeed such a statement could
justify almost any thing university officials might choose
to do. Yet it has considerable merit in light of present day
support for the arts and humanities on many campuses
despite the widespread notion that degrees in those fields
are not so marketable as degrees in areas like business and
computer science. Apparently the president of the University of Oregon did not perceive a need for a library
school in his state.[33] In fact, the closing of a library
school

> appears to result from the belief that
> it can be accomplished without
> doing serious harm to the parent
> institution through a loss of prestige,
> and without inflaming influential
> alumni or legislators.[34]

Demand as characterized in the model is determined by a program's enrollment and by success of its
graduates in the job market. Perceived lack of demand for
librarians in Oregon militated against the survival of the
state's only M.L.S. program. Although the employment
market for holders of the M.L.S. degree did suffer during
periods of economic hardship during the 1970s (although
perhaps not so much as those for humanities graduates),
placement opportunities for new M.L.S graduates have
recently improved.[35] With some notable exceptions,
however, overall enrollment in library schools has declined.[36] White has applied the term "critical mass" to the
point in terms of enrollment (and faculty size and institutional support) below which quality and diversity of
library education becomes impossible to maintain.[37] Evidence obtained from case studies on college closings
suggests that loss of enrollment was indeed a bellwether of
decline at troubled schools.[38]

Locational Advantage for Vanderbilt, for example,
meant the geographic, demographic, and cultural benefits
of locating a specific program in Nashville. For library
education programs location can deliver both geographic
and demographic advantages and disadvantages. Eshelman
points out that "with falling enrollments library educators
stand to benefit from fewer schools in their own geographic area."[39] Five library schools currently serve the
New York metropolitan area; North Carolina has three
M.L.S. granting institutions; and Denton, Texas, has two.
The significance of locational advantage for library
schools, while not entirely clear, can perhaps best be
translated into the idea of competition between neighboring programs as described by Mingle above.[40]

Cost Revenue Relationships and Cost Implications,
items six and seven in the Vanderbilt model, have been
collapsed into one for the purposes of this study. It is
virtually a given that retrenchment in higher education
stems to a degree from financial hardship; it would stand
to reason then that programs determined to be financially
exigent do not endure. Yet examples of small or elite non-
cost efficient, non-cost effective programs abound in colleges and universities, programs that are operated regardless of their revenue-producing capabilities. Thus to
conclude that library schools are closed solely for fiscal
reasons may be too simplistic. Even though demonstrable
evidence of a financial crisis may exist, White contends
that

> the problem is not now, nor has it
> ever really been, one of money.
> University administrators have bud-
> get difficulties, but the level of
> library school expenditure is trivial
> and is not the cause of that diffi-
> culty, nor will cutting or eliminating
> the program solve [administrators']
> problems...If [administrators]

> threaten to cut or eliminate, it is not
> because of a need to preserve
> money. It is because of the need to
> make a political gesture, and the
> perception that cutting or eliminat-
> ing library [school] programs is an
> acceptable sacrifical action, either
> because it is assumed that nobody
> will care, or because the university
> will be little affected, or both of
> these.[41]

Mingle and Associates have suggested by means of
the Vanderbilt Model as one example that retrenchment
can be managed so that programs need not be sacrificed as
political gestures or merely in response to an urge to "do
something" as a show of an administration's good intentions
to save money.

It has been noted that academic program evaluation
often accompanies retrenchment. The body of literature
on program evaluation in higher education has grown large
during the past two decades. One or several more general
evaluation models could have been used as the theoretical
context of the study, but it was chosen instead to concen-
trate on the narrower focus which the literature on retrenchment provides.

OBJECTIVES

Because it departs from available related research
by investigating a single institutional unit and a professional one at that, the study is an exploratory one. Its
objectives are broad and open-ended: first, to identify
conditions which may be related to library school closings;
and to determine the possible existence of a pattern of

predisposing factors across the four programs that have been studied by means of the case method.

The theoretical context poses a number of problem areas subsumed under the first objective. Stated as questions, those include:

1. Was there evidence of an institutional financial crisis which called into question the future of academic programs including the Master of Library Science?

2. Were university administrators familiar with the mission, programs, and *raison d'etre* of the library school?

3. Did university administrators perceive a need for a library school on the campus?

4. Did the Master of Library Science program meet the 1972 Standards promulgated by the Committee on Accreditation of the American Library Association?

5. Did university administrators entertain alternatives other than closing the library school?

6. Was there an accredited M.L.S. program in the same state or region, or one nearby that extended in-state fee courtesy to out-of-state students?

While the theoretical context of the study does suggest the above problem areas--and others which have little or no theoretical base as well--virtually nothing systematic is known about library school closings. Even the facts surrounding the events are unclear. Thus it was anticipated that in the course of the investigation additional variables might emerge which would properly be included in this and future endeavors toward theory building.

DEFINITIONS

For the purposes of the study, "library school" and "library education program" are similarly defined as academic units of a larger college or university which grant the fifth-year Master of Library Science degree after completion of at least one year of full-time study typically consisting of 36 credit hours, 12 courses, or the equivalent. While the name of the degree may vary from institution to institution, Master of Science, Master of Arts, and Master of Librarianship are some of the variants "Master of Library Science" and "M.L.S." are used to represent all library and information science masters degrees granted by library schools in the United States. A library school that is "closed" or "defunct" is one that has ceased to offer the fifth-year program and has disbanded or is in the throes of doing so.

METHODOLOGY

Rationale

The nature of the problem under investigation is the key variable in choosing a research methodology. The need for a case study arises when

> an empirical inquiry must examine a
> contemporary phenomenon in its real
> life context, especially when the
> boundaries between phenomenon and
> context are not clearly evident.[42]

Such detailed observations as case studies provide are especially useful in documenting decisions occurring over a period of time with no clear beginning or end points and whose implications are perhaps too complex for single factor theories.

Yin rejects the stereotypes commonly associated with case studies: that they lead only to unconfirmable conclusions and are a method of last resort. Stereotypes not withstanding, observes Yin, case studies seem to be appearing with increasing frequency.[43] A June 1985 piece in the "Scholarship" column of *The Chronicle of Higher Education* hailed a new mode of inquiry favoring interpretation over strictly scientific, quantitative approaches. "The challenge to scientific positivism is not just occurring in the social sciences," observed one researcher:

> It is part of a glacial shift in modern thought, away from older certitudes, and even from the very quest for certainty....Even in the sciences, some people like Thomas Kuhn are arguing that the scientific mode of inquiry is not completely objective.[44]

The singular attractiveness of case studies lies in their strong potential for theory building. Miles and Huberman have commented that

> qualitative data are attractive. They are a source of well-grounded, rich descriptions and explanations of processes occurring in local contexts....Then too, qualitative data are more likely to lead to serendipitous findings and to new theoretical integrations: they help researchers go beyond initial preconceptions and frameworks [45]

Yet other objections have been voiced as well. Perhaps foremost among those is case studies' uncertain validity, the systematic biasing effect statistically related to non-random error that prevents indicators from measuring the theoretical concept as they are intended.[46]

External validity--whether or not findings are generalizable beyond the immediate case(s)--is of prime concern in the present study. In contrast to survey research where a properly drawn sample generalizes to a much larger population, Yin maintains that

> [the] analogy to samples and universes is incorrect when dealing with case studies,....because survey research relies on statistical generalization, whereas case studies rely on analytical generalization.[47]

Theoretical sampling, a term used by Glaser and Strauss, describes the process of collecting data where the researcher strives to generalize specific findings to some broader theory.[48] In the context of the present study, that theory is retrenchment in higher education. External validity is assessed by replicability: "the more variations in places, people, and procedures a piece of research can withstand and still yield the same findings, the more externally valid the conclusions."[49]

Internal validity is said to be present when it accurately identifies causal relationships. Goldhor has written,

> [the case study] maximizes validity by increasing the number of variables on which information is secured and by the depth of analysis it tends to produce, especially with regard to an understanding of the pattern of cause and effect.[50]

Even Backstrom and Hursh-Cesar in their text on survey research acknowledge that potential in the case study.[51] It should be noted, however, that the determination of causal relationships was not the primary goal of the present study; rather, the objective has been to identify conditions that precluded and coincided with library school closings with an aim toward reporting those and subsequently comparing conditions at four universities.

Criterion or predictive validity "is at issue when the purpose is to use an instrument to estimate some important form of behavior that is...referred to as the criterion."[52] Criterion validity, a function of the extent of the correspondence between the test and the criterion, is established when the dependent variable has been fully operationalized and precisely measured, and the results successfully replicated. Yet Carmines and Zeller have reservations about the applicability of criterion validity to the social sciences, for in their view there simply do not exist a large number of relevant criterion variables from which to choose.[53]

In reviewing recent thoughts on the subject of construct validity, Miles and Huberman concluded that some researchers have shied away from the problem altogether, on the grounds that unequivocal determination of the validity of findings is impossible; as "there is no social reality 'out there' to be accounted for."[54] In their view,

> social processes...are ephemeral, fluid
> phenomena with no existence inde-
> pendent of social actors' ways of
> construing and describing them.[55]

There can be no doubt that much remains to be written about the applicability of validity to case study methodology. Recent efforts like that of Miles and Huberman exemplify trends in that direction. If Yin's suspicion is correct--that is, if case studies are enjoying renewed popularity and wider, more imaginative use--additional new concepts and procedures will evolve.

Reliability--stability, accuracy, and precision of measurement--is also a formidable problem faced by the researcher. Reliability is "the extent to which a measuring procedure yields the same results on repeated trials."[56] Statistically, random error is inversely related to reliability; in other words, the more random error present, the lower the reliability of a measurement. While high reliability does not unequivocally guarantee consistent results (for random error is always present to some degree), low reliability is certain to guarantee inconsistent results. Carmines and Zeller stress that repeated measures "never precisely duplicate one another, but they do tend to be consistent."[57]

Thus minimizing bias is the researcher's goal. Reliability checks for survey instruments are well-documented and procedures codified. Since the potential for bias is so much greater where case studies are concerned, however, and since random error present in case studies cannot be mathematically determined, a means for maximizing the reliability of the present study was sought. Yin has proposed one. All procedures followed should be documented in what he terms a case study protocol in order to operationalize and describe as many steps as fully as possible. Such a protocol might be thought of as a kind of audit trail to be followed by future replicators.[58]

Miles and Huberman have set new standards for ensuring reliability, in addition to their underscoring the importance of establishing an audit trail, by advocating an interactive data analysis model consisting of four components--data collection, data reduction, data display, and conclusion drawing/verifying.[59]

Data Analysis

One characteristic of the present study which precluded survey research is that the data sought and obtained
do not easily fit into discrete categories which the effective
use of a measuring instrument demands. Some quantitative
data have been collected (enrollment totals and budgetary
figures, for example), however, as a means of organizing
and analyzing the vast amounts of qualitative data gathered
in the course of the 1985 site visits.

In *The Discovery of Grounded Theory: Strategies
for Qualitative Research*, Glaser and Strauss discuss theoretical sampling to collect *slices of data* [italics theirs],
"different views or vantage points from which to understand a category and to develop its properties...."[60] Category development is the goal, and as comparing categories'
differences generates properties about them, most any slice
of data yields some social-structural information. In comparative analysis, conflicting slices of data are not seen as
tests of one another but as different modes of knowing,
enriching rather than disproving one another.[61]

The existing theory of retrenchment in higher education has provided a springboard or stepping stone, a
stimulus that has facilitated the development of relevant
categories. As the objectives of the study grew from
existing theory, so did the categories for comparative
analysis. Their relationship is displayed below.

Objective	Category
1. Evidence of a financial crisis at the institution	1. Budgetary figures, documentary evidence, informants' assessments
2. Administrators' familiarity with mission and goals of library school	2. Administrators' statements, documentary evidence
3. Need for a library school	3. Informants' statements, documentary evidence
4. Compliance with stanards for accreditation	4. COA reports, informants' statements
5. Demographic factors	5. Documentary evidence
6. Alternate options, other programs closed	6. Documentary evidence, informants' statements

The next step, the constant comparative method of analysis as formulated by Glaser and Strauss, is concerned with generating and plausibly suggesting (but not provisionally testing) many categories and properties and has four stages:

> 1. Comparing incidents applicable to each category,
> 2. integrating categories and then properties,
> 3. delimiting the theory, and
> 4. writing the theory.[62]

Inductive in approach, the constant comparative method tends to result in developmental, rather than static, theory. Certainly given the possibly evolutionary aspects of library school closings, that method of comparison and analysis has considerable salience to the present study.

PROCEDURES

Subjects and Informants

Twelve accredited M.L.S. programs have been disbanded since the late 1970s. While studying one closing in depth would have been desirable from the dual standpoints of simplicity and thoroughness, results obtained would not have satisfied objective two of the study: to compare possible predisposing conditions and to determine whether patterns could be identified.

Library schools that have closed within the past several years were more desirable as subjects since the principals involved (university administrators, deans or directors, and faculty) were more likely still to be *in situ*. Barring from the study the first few schools that closed, however, may have ruled out an issue that was not addressed but nevertheless warrants mention and consideration in further research: was date of closing a key variable? In other words, were the programs terminated in the years 1978 through 1981, for example, closed for the same reasons as those which have ceased operation since 1982?

Four library schools, two public and two private, were selected for study. Despite the fact that investigating the closing of library schools at publicly supported versus privately supported institutions was not an objective of the study, comparisons beg to be made, if only to lay to rest questions that might be raised *post hoc* from research examining more public closings than private.

The schools are neither identified nor the informants named, for it was believed that assured of anonymity, principals involved would be more likely to speak freely and candidly to the author; that suspicion was borne out many times over. Some readers will undoubtedly find it tempting to try to guess which four closings have been described. Although such speculation is certainly the prerogative of those persons, it will not be joined by the author. In the interests of anonymity, the four schools have been named Alpha, Beta, Gamma, and Delta, and informants have been given generic titles. That is, all chief academic officers, whether officially titled vice president for academic affairs, for example, or dean of academic affairs (two commonly used titles), have been designated as chief academic officer or simply vice president; library school heads, known on their campuses as deans, directors, or chairpersons, have been designated as executive officers; faculty have retained that title, as have practicing librarians (or practitioners) and students.

A letter explaining the stated objectives of the study, requesting permission for a personal tape recorded interview, and assuring anonymity, was sent to each present or former executive officer along with an abstract of the research proposal and a copy of the author's *vita*. The executive officers were asked to name other university administrator(s) who figured prominently in the decision to terminate the four programs. Subsequent letters were sent to those persons, explaining the study and asking to arrange appointments at the same time the visit to the library school was made. A letter of endorsement signed by the dean of the School of Library and Information Science at Indiana University was included with each request.

Initial letters of inquiry to executive officers were mailed the last week of May 1985. By mid-July all four of those individuals had responded favorably, granting the author permission to visit each school within the several months that would follow. As key university administrators had been willingly identified by the executive officers, a second mailing then took place; again including an explanatory letter signed by the author, a seconding letter signed by the dean of the School of Library and information Science, an abstract of the research proposal, and the author's *vita*. In two cases, a third round of letters was mailed to faculty, seeking their participation and ascertaining their availability for late summer or early autumn interviews. Precise appointment times were subsequently scheduled by telephone during late July and early August. Between August 5 and September 26, 1985, and in April of 1986, the author made six site-visits to four universities. In two of the cases, visits occupied periods of four days per school; scheduling problems necessitated brief second visits in the other two cases. Thirty-one persons were interviewed at the four library schools.

The Interview

Matarazzo utilized the focused interview in eliciting from his respondents detailed information about special library closings. Mitroff has thus characterized the focused interview:

> In the focused interview, the interview questions that are asked of each subject are relatively formalized (standardized), while the question asking procedure is relatively unstructured (open-ended) and thus somewhat variable from subject to subject.[63]

That technique enabled Matarazzo to explore and to develop issues raised in the course of the interview that might not have arisen had he used a more closed-ended, structured approach.[64]

Bodgan and Biklen's discussion of the open-ended interview emphasizes that it allows the researcher to

> [probe] more deeply, picking up on
> topics and issues that the respondent
> initiates. The subject plays a
> stronger role in defining the content
> of the interview and the direction of
> the study.[65]

It was further anticipated that such an approach, by permitting flexibility and encouraging spontaneity, would provide insight into how the informants viewed the closing of their schools in addition to securing more factual details from them.

Prior to the visits, background material on each library school was gathered from catalogs and bulletins, the *ALA Yearbook*, and other sources. The annual statistical reports of the Association for Library and Information Science Education (ALISE) were used to obtain retrospective demographic and enrollment data.

Campus newspapers, a prime source of documentary evidence, were made available to the author at all four universities. Those provided background information both on the closings and on historical circumstances which may have precipitated each one. Upon arrival at the campuses, newspapers were examined at length before interviewing commenced. University archives, special collections, and many of the informants themselves generously provided documentation both public and confidential; typical varieties included minutes of faculty meetings, minutes of boards of trustees, university memoranda concerning cutbacks and realignment, COA self-study documents and subsequent COA reports, and library school proposals for reallocating priorities.

The majority of the interviews occupied roughly one hour's time; sessions with a few key informants lasted from one-and-a-half to two hours, however. Parallel collection techniques were used; in addition to tape recording each interview, the author took longhand notes in order to capture significant points and to record additional questions that arose during the conversation.

RELATED RESEARCH

Library school closings as a topic for discussion first appeared in the literature during the summer of 1983 with the publication of two speculative pieces. The first, by Dyer and O'Connor entitled "Crisis in Library Education," boldly declared that library schools were indeed in a state of crisis brought about by the dual threat of institutional retrenchment, when library schools can be targets for elimination, and by the sharply declining number of students who were seeking the M.L.S., a 40 percent drop in the previous eight years. The schools in trouble, Dyer and O'Connor alleged, were "characterized by poor morale, inability to secure outside funding, and declining university support."[66] In their view, entrepreneurial activities-- public relations, politicking, and grantsmanship--may make the difference between a healthy program and one that eventually becomes a sitting duck. And it is only librarians and library educators who "have the ability to recast the professional training of librarians for either survival or elimination."[67]

One point Dyer and O'Connor failed to make was made the next month in *Library Journal* by Eshelman, who implied that there were then too many M.L.S. programs for the number of students who desired the degree; some 30 new programs sprang up and were duly accredited during the populous, prosperous 1960s.[68] Bidlack supported that contention as well.[69] The winnowing of the marketplace,

Eshelman wrote, was at work; "six to eight" programs would be phased out or relocated at the the undergraduate level within two years.[70]

The effects on a program of loss of accreditation are less clear. While White[71] sees no relationship between "quality" and termination and Eshelman[72] acknowledges only a tenuous one, Dyer and O'Connor have contended that

>   the accrediting process brings with it
>   a certain irony: not receiving full
>   accreditation may prompt the uni-
>   versity to examine its need for a li-
>   brary school, but receiving it does
>   not guarantee a secure future. After
>   the library school at [State Univer-
>   sity at New York at] Geneseo was
>   fully reaccredited, it announced that
>   it was closing its doors.[73]

White has written persuasively on a number of occasions concerning the requirements for excellence in library education. His widely quoted notion of "critical mass" is perhaps even more compelling today than when it first appeared in print in 1979.[74]

Some of the ideas he put forth in a 1983 *Journal of Education for Librarianship* piece slightly predated Dyer and O'Connor; and although accreditation was his subject, his ideas bear directly on library school closings. Some of those were quoted in a previous section of this paper. One that warrants repeating in part, however, is

>   the problem is not now, nor has it
>   ever been, one of money....The level
>   of library school expenditure is
>   trivial and is not the cause of
>   [budget] difficulty, nor will cutting

or eliminating the program solve
[administrators'] problems....The
elimination of library education
appears to result from the belief that
it can be accomplished without
doing serious harm to the parent
institution.[75]

Matarazzo's study, "Closing the Corporate Library:
Case Studies on the Decision-Making Process," merits
attention chiefly because of one of its key findings:
corporate libraries were closed that lacked a champion in
upper management to serve as an advocate by making
known to corporate decision makers the library's organiza-
tion-wide contributions. If the library were considered
essential at the highest levels, decision makers in the event
of a fiscal emergency would be less disposed to curtail library service or to suspend it altogether.[76]

In other words, Matarazzo's findings illustrate the
need for "friends in high places." While special libraries
and library education programs are notably different in
terms of mission, type of financial support, institutional
placement, and organizational characteristics, the two exhibit one remarkable similarity: their roles and functions
are often misunderstood and disregarded by outsiders who
possess the potential to eliminate them because of that
ignorance. Thus it may be incumbent upon library school
deans, as it was in Matarazzo's view of special librarians,
continually to justify their programs' existence and make
known to university administrators the programs' significance to the campus, to library education, and to society at
large.

Recently there appeared in *American Libraries* "The
Anatomy of a Library School Shutdown" by Seelmeyer, a
journalist assigned to report on the closing of the Graduate
School of Librarianship and Information Management at
the University of Denver. His tale is one fraught with

evident misunderstanding, disagreement, and poor communication among the parties involved. He concluded that

> the experience of the University of
> Denver library school shows what
> can happen when a library education
> program doesn't get a chance to
> present its case to a university
> administration bent on re-
> organization...and when a library
> school is shut out of deliberations
> about a university's future.[77]

Whether friends in high places might have pled the Denver school's case remains a matter for conjecture. Seelmeyer's contribution to the literature on library school closings should not be dismissed as one journalist's completion of an assigned task. Rather, "The Anatomy of a Library School Shutdown" merits note as the first published account of a closing. Even without scholarly trappings, the Seelmeyer article will be widely cited.

Discussing the creation and abolition of new departments in his study, *The Organization of Academic Work*, Blau has noted that abolishing old departments and establishing new ones must be a continuing process:

> The abolishment of departments that
> have become obsolete probably fur-
> nishes a more severe test of the
> flexibility of the organization than
> does the creation of new ones,
> because the elimination of depart-
> ments directly conflicts with vested
> interests.[78]

Blau found that the size of an academic institution is unrelated to the likelihood that departments would be done away with($r=-.04$, $n=102$). Nevertheless two conditions were determined to affect elimination of old departments. Centralization was one: Blau found that decentralization promoted overall structural flexibility, whereas centralization had a negative effect on it. Thus he concluded, the greater the centralized authority over expenditure of funds a president held, the less likely it was that departments had recently been abolished(r=-.28, n=102, p<.01). Moreover, schools located in the Southern part of the United States abolished departments less frequently than did institutions elsewhere in the nation (r=-.34, n=102,p<.01), a finding Blau does not fully explain since he also discovered that Southern institutions were not appreciably less likely to have created new departments; and the variable, South, he found to be only trivially correlated with presidential authority over expenditures (r=-.06, n=102).[79]

College closings from the mid-1970s onward spawned numerous case study investigations. A worthy example is Beeman's "Wilson College: A Case Study," prepared for a Lilly Endowment seminar in the autumn of 1979. The Pennsylvania women's college's predicament received widespread press coverage earlier that year when a court-ordered mandate removed two trustees, including the president of Bryn Mawr College, and enjoined the closing of the college without prior court approval. Unquestionably, declining enrollment and subsequent budgetary shortfalls were at the root of Wilson's troubles, which neither aggressive fund raising nor extended recruiting could ameliorate. A group of vocal alumnae spearheaded a "Save Wilson" campaign which Beeman acknowledged to be effective, although she only barely manages to conceal her disapprobation of many of the group's tactics (threatening and obscene telephone calls to the president, for example).[80]

Hammond's "Organizational Response for Survival: A Case Study in Higher Education," describes the survival efforts of Cazenovia College, a two year liberal arts college for women, whose closing was announced in 1974. Once

again an *ad hoc* group was instrumental in keeping Cazenovia open; and a "business model," patterned after a highly
successful revitalization carried out by then president John
C. Sawhill at New York University, was implemented for
governance of the college.[81]

A third case study, an evaluation of the adminis-
trative and decision making structures of Fontbonne
College in St. Louis, is notable for its methodology and
framework, the Academic Institution-Building Model
(AIBM), developed by the Institution Research Group at
Indiana University. According to project director
Chamberlain,

> the AIBM is a strategic planning
> model [allowing] for an institution to
> be viewed within a given time di-
> mension and within the context of
> the environment from which it
> derives its meaning and existence.[82]

Assessment of administrative decision making and
efficiency is made on nine variables--five institution
variables and four environmental linkages. Chamberlain
and his associates found that Fontbonne, previously faced
with an institutional identity crisis which precipitated the
study, had every reason to continue operation provided
that certain modifications in governance, financing, structure, and self-development were made. That the AIBM
incorporates a measuring instrument by means of which
numeric coefficients can be obtained sets it apart from the
more traditional qualitative case study methodologies used
in higher education and would appear to make it an attractive alternative for researchers.

In addition to the three case studies cited above,
several others describe how and why individual colleges
closed and deserve brief mention. Studies by Borton and
Whalen on Newton College of the Sacred Heart,[83] by Mil-

lett on ten college mergers that took place in the early
1970s,[84] and by Healy and Peterson[85] have made an important contribution to the literature. Descriptions of
specific college closings were presented in such "how-to-
do-it" pieces as West's "The Right Way to Close,"[86]
Willmer and O'Connor's "Closing a College with Compassion,"[87] and McIntyre's "Preparing for College Closings."[88]
Those and other similar articles actually contain little
descriptive material, prescribing instead specific measures
to be taken in closing as effectively and humanely as possible. Finally, Miller and Erwin's "Analysis of College
Closings" applied a model of industrial plant closings to the
literature of college closings and identified what the inves-
tigators deemed to be most of the elements involved in the
closing process. The model's strength would appear to be
that it fulfills a need for systematic, analytical studies of
groups of closings.[89]

   A pair of the most widely cited papers in cutback
management was published by Levine in *Public Administration Review* in 1978 and 1979. The author used a
four-cell matrix to explain the causes of public organizations' decline as external, internal, political, or eco-
nomic/technical, concluding that after decades of growth,
organizations and their managers are at an embryonic state
insofar as cutback management is concerned.[90,91] In his
study of public cutback management Stefonek discussed
both public and private program termination, borrowing
from the work of the eminent organization theorist Cyert,
to review private terminations. The vicious circle of
enrollment decline which leads to financial difficulty
leading to further decline, and so forth, can be broken by
the infusion of additional resources; that is not so easily
accomplished, however, since dwindling external resources
may have been the initial cause of the decline.[92] The best
answer, Cyert contended, is improved internal management, despite the fact that "academics resist being managed
by expert managers, and they seek to have one of their
own kind in top management positions."[93]

Quoted extensively in a previous part of this paper was *The Challenges of Retrenchment* by Mingle and Associates, a major work dealing with a wide range of retrenchment related issues.[94] Similarly, *Reallocation*, published by the National Association of College and University Business Officers and also previously cited, described strategies for resource management employed successfully by ten colleges and universities.[95]

The body of periodical literature on educational retrenchment is vast and growing. A recent online search of the ERIC database, inputting only the statement RETRENCHMENT/MAJ AND HIGHER EDUCATION/ MAJ (MAJ indicating major descriptors) turned up some 120 postings since the year 1976. Without limiting to major descriptors the number of documents retrieved for the same time period numbered nearly 600. Not all of the 600 or even the 120 were relevant to the current study, but a sampling of items reveals the following trends.

It is widely agreed that higher education in the United States and other countries--the United Kingdom, Canada, and the Netherlands have also been studied--is indeed in crisis caused largely by declining student populations and financial emergency.[96,97,98] Institutions can emerge from the crisis/opportunity dilemma with aplomb if administrators capitalize upon strengths rather succumbing to weaknesses.[99] And finally, specific strategies of many types are proposed for managing institutions during no-growth periods.[100,101]

REFERENCES

1. William R. Eshelman, "Death at an Early Age: Library Schools in Oregon and California in Jeopardy," *Wilson Library Bulletin* 51(6):794 (June 1977).

2. Esther Dyer and Daniel O'Connor, "Crisis in Library Education," *Wilson Library Bulletin* 57(6):860 (June 1983).

3. Robert D. Stueart, "Great Expectations: Library and Information Science Education at the Crossroads," *Library Journal* 106(18): 1992 (October 15, 1981).

4. Thomas J. Galvin, "Foreword," in Anthony Debons and Donald W. King, *The Information Professional: Survey of an Emerging Field* (New York: Marcel Dekker, 1981), pp.iii-iv.

5. José-Marie Griffiths, "Microcomputers and On line Activities," *ASIS Bulletin* 10(4):13 -14 (April 1984).

6. Association for Library and Information Science Education, *Library and Information Science Education Statistical Report 1984* (State College: ALISE, 1984). p. S-21.

7. American Association of Library Schools, *Library Education Statistical Report 1980* (State College: ALISE, 1980), p. S-26.

8. Carol L. Learmont and Stephen Van Houten, "Placements & Salaries 1983: Catching Up," *Library Journal* 109(17): 1805 (October 15, 1983).

9. Dyer and O'Connor, p. 863.

10. James R. Mingle, "Choices Facing Higher Education in the 1980s," in James R. Mingle and Associates, *The Challenges of Retrenchment* (San Francisco: Jossey-Bass, 1981), p. 350.

11. James R. Mingle, "Challenges of Retrenchment," in James R. Mingle and Associates *The Challenges of Retrenchment* (San Francisco: Jossey-Bass, 1981), p. 1.

12. James R. Mingle and Donald M. Norris, "Institutional Strategies for Responding to Decline," in James R. Mingle and Asociates *The Challenges of Retrenchment* (San Francisco: Jossey-Bass, 1981), p. 47.

13. Mingle and Norris, p. 52.

14. Mingle and Norris, p. 52.

15. Mingle and Norris, p. 52.

16. Charles R. McClure, "The Planning Process: Strategies for Change," *College and Research Libraries* 39:456 (November 1978).

17. Mingle and Norris, pp. 56-57.

18. David L. Clark, "In Consideration of Goal-Free Planning: The Failure of Traditional Planning Systems in Education," *Educational Administration Quarterly* 17(3):49 (Summer 1981).

19. Clark, p. 50.

20. Mingle and Norris, pp. 59-60.

21. Mingle and Norris, pp. 62-63.

22. Mingle and Norris, p. 63.

23. William R. Eshelman, "The Erosion of Library Education," *Library Journal* 108(6):1309-1312 (July 1983).

24. Matthew B. Miles and A. Michael Huberman, *Qualitative Data Analysis: A Sourcebook of New Methods* (Beverly Hills: Sage Publications, 1984), pp. 28-29.

25. James A. Hyatt et al., *Reallocation; Strategies for Effective Resource Management* (Washington, D.C.: National Association of College and University Business Officers, 1984), p. 2.

26. James M. Matarazzo, "Closing the Corporate Library: Case Studies on the Decision-Making Process," Ph.D. Dissertation, University of Pittsburgh, 1979, p. 132.

27. Herbert S. White, "Accreditation and the Pursuit of Excellence," *Journal of Education for Librarianship* 23(4):255 (Spring 1983).

28. White, p. 254.

29. White, p. 254.

30. White, pp. 254-255.

31. Eshelman, "The Erosion of Library Education," p. 1311.

32. Mingle and Norris, pp. 62-63.

33. Eshelman, "Death at an Early Age," p. 794.

34. White, p. 255.

35. Learmont and Van Houten, "Placements and Salaries 1983,"p. 1805.

36. Eshelman, "The Erosion of Library Education," p. 1311.

37. Herbert S. White, "Critical Mass for Library Education," *American Libraries* 10(8):479 (September 1979).

38. Alice L. Beeman, "Wilson College: A Case Study," (Paper delivered at a Lilly Endowment Seminar for Indiana Independent Colleges and Universities, Indianapolis, October 10, 1979), p. 7.

39. Eshelman, "The Erosion of Library Education," p. 1309.

40. Mingle, p. 350.

41. White, "Accreditation and the Pursuit of Excellence," pp. 261-262.

42. Robert K. Yin, "The Case Study as a Serious Research Methodology," *Knowledge: Creation, Diffusion, Utilization* 3(1): 98 (September 1981).

43. Yin, p. 97.

44. Karen J. Winkler, "Questioning the Science in Social Science, Scholars Signal a 'Turn to Interpretation,'" *The Chronicle of Higher Education* 30(17): 5-6 (June 26, 1985).

45. Miles and Huberman, p. 15.

46. Robert K. Yin, *Case Study Research: Design and Methods* (Beverly Hills: Sage, 1984), p. 39.

47. Yin, Case Study Research, p. 39.

48. Barney G. Glaser and Anselm L. Strauss, *The Discovery of Grounded Theory: Strategies for Qualitative Research* (New York: Aldine, 1967), p. 45.

49. Louise H. Kidder, *Research Methods in Social Relations*, 4th ed. (New York: Holt, Rinehart, & Winston, 1981), p. 8.

50. Herbert Goldhor, *An Introduction to Scientific Research in Librarianship* (Urbana: University of Illinois Graduate School of Library Science, 1972), p. 128.

51. Charles H. Backstrom and Gerald Hursh-Cesar, *Survey Research*, 2nd. ed. (New York: John Wiley & Sons, 1981), p. 11.

52. J.C. Nunnally, *Psychometric Theory* (New York: McGraw-Hill, 1978), p. 87.

53. Edward G. Carmines and Richard A. Zeller, *Reliability and Validity Assessment* (Beverly Hills: Sage, 1979), p. 19.

54. Miles and Huberman, p. 16.

55. Miles and Huberman, p. 16.

56. Carmines and Zeller, p. 11.

57. Carmines and Zeller, p. 12.

58. Yin, *Case Study Research*, pp. 39-40.

59. Miles and Huberman, pp. 21-23.

60. Glaser and Strauss, p. 65.

61. Glaser and Strauss, pp. 68-69.

62. Glaser and Strauss, pp. 104-115.

63. Ian I. Mitroff, *The Subjective Side of Science* (Amsterdam: Elsevier, 1974), p. 39.

64. Matarazzo, pp. 14-15.

65. Robert C. Bogdan and Sari Knopp Biklen, *Qualitative Research for Education: An Introduction to Theory and Methods* (Boston: Allyn and Bacon, 1982), p. 136.

66. Dyer and O'Connor, p. 863.

67. Dyer and O'Connor, p. 863.

68. Eshelman, "The Erosion of Library Education," p. 1310.

69. Russell E. Bidlack, Report to the Dean of the Graduate School of Indiana University, mimeographed, 1985, p. 3.

70. Eshelman, "The Erosion of Library Education," p. 1311.

71. White, "Accreditation and the Pursuit of Excellence," p. 254.

72. Eshelman, "The Erosion of Library Education," p. 1310.

73. Dyer and O'Connor, p. 862.

74. White, "Critical Mass for Library Education," p. 479.

75. White, "Accreditation and the Pursuit of Excellence," pp.255, 261-262.

76. Matarazzo, pp. 138-139.

77. John Seelmeyer, "The Anatomy of a Library School Shutdown," *American Libraries* 16(2): 113 (February 1985).

78. Peter M. Blau, *The Organization of Academic Work* (New York: John Wiley & Sons, 1973), p. 208.

79. Blau, pp. 211-212.

80. Beeman, pp. 32-34.

81. Martine F. Hammond, "Organizational Response for Survival: A Case Study in Higher Education," (Paper delivered at the Annual Meeting of the Association for the Study of Higher Education, Washington, D.C., March 3-4, 1981), pp. 8-20.

82. Philip C. Chamberlain, "An Assessment of the Administrative and Decision Making Structures of Fontbonne College," mimeographed, 1983, p. 4.

83. W.W. Borton and J.J. Whalen, untitled manuscript, 1981.

84. J.D. Millett, *Mergers in Higher Education: An Analysis of Ten Case Studies* (Washington, D.C.: American Council on Education, 1976).

85. R.M. Healy and V.T. Peterson, "Trustees and College Failure:A Study of the Role of the Board in Four Small College Terminations," mimeographed, 1976.

86. T.W. West, "The Right Way to Close," *AGB Reports* July/August 1980, pp. 37-44.

87. W.K. Willmer and M.J. O'Connor, "Closing with Compassion,"_AGB Reports_ November/December 1979, pp. 27-31.

88. K.J.H. McIntyre, "Preparing for College Closing," *Educational Record* Summer 1977, pp. 290-298.

89. James L. Miller and J. Michael Erwin, "Analysis of College Closings," (Paper delivered at the Annual Meeting of the Association for the Study of Higher Education, Washington, D.C., March 2-3, 1982).

90. Charles H. Levine, "Organizational Decline and
    Cutback Management," *Public Administration
    Review* 38(4):316-324 (July/August 1978).

91. Charles H. Levine, "More on Cutback Management:
    Hard Questions for Hard Times," *Public Ad-
    ministration Review* 39(2):179-183 (March/ April
    1979).

92. Tom Stefonek, *Cutback Management in Public Organi-
    zations* (Madison: Wisconsin Department of Public
    Instruction Division for Management, Planning, and
    Federal Services, 1979), p. 28.

93. Stefonek, pp. 28-29.

94. Hyatt et al.

95. Mingle and Associates.

96. Jerome M. Deutsch, "Retrenchment: Crisis or Chal-
    lenge," *Educational Record* 64(1):41-44 (Winter
    1983).

97. Cynthia Hardy, "The Management of University Cut-
    backs: Politics, Planning, and Participation,"
    Canadian Journal of Higher Education 14(1):59-69
    (Winter 1984).

98. Carol Frances, "The Financial Resilience of American
    Colleges and Universities," *New Directions for
    Higher Education* no. 38 (Successful Responses to
    Financial Difficulty) 10(2):113-120 (June 1982).

99. Deutsch, p. 44.

100. George B. Weathersby, "Scarce Resources Can Be a
     Golden Opportunity for Higher Education," Change
     14(2):12-13 (March 1982).

101. K.J. Doyle, "Managing Higher Education in a Climate of Contraction: A Conceptual Model," *Journal of Tertiary Educational Administration* 2(2):139-149 October 1980)

CHAPTER 2

FOUR CASE STUDIES

Data collected in the course of the author's interviews with library educators and university administrators, and from the examination of documentary evidence provided by the informants and others, have been put into narrative form as case study reports on the closings of the four library schools. In order to preserve the anonymity of the informants who gave so freely of their time, the universities have been named Alpha University, the University of Beta, Gamma University, and the University of Delta.

ALPHA UNIVERSITY

Since its beginnings during the Great Depression, the library school at Alpha University had served a constituency far more diverse than its founders perhaps anticipated when they set out to provide education for public and school librarians in a region where such programs were few. Many of its nearly 5,000 alumni occupied positions of visibility throughout the profession. Future librarians came to Alpha from all over the United States and a host of foreign countries. On a campus where a college of arts and sciences numbered some 4,000 students, the library school was one of a handful of professional programs-- along with social work, nursing, business administration, and law--in which the university took great pride. Plans to close the library school were announced in the summer of 1984. "We were losing a bundle on it," said the president.

Alpha University had ridden the crest of the postwar baby boom. At its peak in the late 1960s and early 1970s, enrollment had swelled with undergraduates seeking a liberal arts education in a congenial social environment. Accompanying the record enrollment were a variety of new programs, additional faculty appointments, and an expansion of the physical plant. But by the early 1980s the baby boom had graduated and Alpha found itself perilously close to financial disaster. The university's budget deficit, estimated in 1984 at $2.5 million out of total expenditures of $75 million, was projected to reach $6 million by the end of the 1984-85 academic year. Total enrollment in the autumn of 1984 represented the fourth decrease in as many years; from 1983 to 1984 alone, Alpha's enrollment dropped from 8,885 to 8,034, for a one-year decline of 9.6 percent. Moreover, an analysis of undergraduate attrition revealed that between 50 and 60 percent of the freshmen did not return for their sophomore year. Said one university official,

> It shakes you up when you realize
> that of those who entered as fresh-
> men, four years later less than 30
> percent were graduating from here.
> It's hard to know where they went....
> Monetary factors? There was no
> question about that.

In January of 1984 the president was fired after a five-year tenure and his replacement was promoted from within--from the faculty of the college of arts and sciences. In a memorandum to the Board of Trustees, the new president stated that

> much evidence exists to suggest that
> we have not been fulfilling our basic
> obligations to students as we should
> have and that this failure is one of
> the root causes of our current
> financial problem...One can name
> many of the categories in which
> such evidence is extant.

He identified six categories, including the following:

> 1. A 'volatile enrollment situation' caused in part because Alpha is a 'safety net school' for many prospective students. 'As institutions of greater prestige dip into their waiting lists because of student demographics, this university is experiencing erosion in its cache of "deposited" students late in the spring.' And shortfalls in enrollment contributed to financial problems.
>
> 2. The university had 'frittered away major grants' in recent years.
>
> 3. National prestige in only a few academic areas. 'The undergraduate programs mostly lack distinction.'
>
> 4. A high undergraduate attrition rate: much higher than any of Alpha's 'imagined peer group.'
>
> 5. Runaway administrative and financial aid costs. He estimated that it cost the university almost $3,200 to enroll each undergraduate student, nearly half of whom leave before graduating. 'We are substantially discounting our product.'
>
> 6. 'Fundamental problems in undergraduate education and its image, ironically the budget base of the university.'

Concluded the president, "it is abundantly clear that major changes in our undergraduate programs and their marketing are indicated."

The library school, along with its counterparts across the nation, had enjoyed its own period of growth and prosperity during the 1960s and 70s. The M.A. in librarianship, updated to include an information management component, emphasized, according to the bulletin, "the nature and function of information services and the way in which information is processed." Encouraged to develop a specialization during the 60 quarter-hour program, students could choose from among over 40 courses. The separately accredited Master of Law Librarianship (M.L.L.) and the dual M.L.L.-Juris Doctor degree, both offered in cooperation with Alpha's law school, were widely respected. A second dual degree program was established with the history department: after six quarters a student could earn both the M.A. in librarianship and the M.A. in history and archives.

The number of special programs sponsored by the library school grew as well, to include a media specialist concentration within the M.A.; a non-degree educational media specialist endorsement for holders of master's degrees in education or allied fields; an elementary school media endorsement for elementary school teachers; specialties in archives administration and law librarianship, both within the M.A.; a certificate of advanced study for mid-career professionals; and a cooperative doctoral program in which students pursuing the terminal degree in another school or department could receive elective credit for as many as 45 quarter hours of library school course work.

With the initiation in the winter term of 1983 of a non-degree certificate in information management, the library school--which had undergone a name change shortly after the arrival of a new executive officer two years previously--appeared to have positioned itself firmly in the information age, in response to a demand for what the bulletin cites is a "new breed" of information professional, and had put into place the first phase of a comprehensive plan to establish a College of Information Management. The non-degree program, offered first at the request of the president, who had asked for proof of the level of interest in information management before proceeding further, attracted 82 new non-matriculated adult students; the first three certificates were granted a year later.

The second phase, a concentration in information management within the M.A., (the new degree, Master of Arts in Information Resources Management, or MAIRM) was begun in the fall term of 1983: approximately 15 students would be enrolled in the first MAIRM class and they would graduate during the 1985-1986 academic year. Of that number, several were previously-enrolled M.A. students who had applied for admission to MAIRM.

As detailed in the document which proposed it to Alpha's president, the College of Information Management was designed to provide an understanding of "how information is created and produced; how information is used by people and machines; how information is organized, controlled, and acquired; how information is stored and retrieved; [and] how information is managed and marketed."

Organizations sending their employees to Alpha could hope to realize "increased productivity because of better, more accurate information; reduced costs for retrieving information; better use of existing information systems; better decisions concerning the acquisition of new information systems; [and] reduced travel and conference costs through improved use of telecommunications." The new curriculum included graduate courses in such subjects as economics of information, systems analysis and design, telecommunications, records management, database management, human factors in information systems, information policy, and an opportunity for internship in an information management function. Serving on an advisory panel which aided the library school's executive officer in developing the program were some 20 information workers representing local commerce and industry. Aggressively the new program was promoted--to prospective students via an elaborate mailing campaign, to practicing information professionals in the area, and to faculty and students in other schools and departments on Alpha's campus.

Formally proposed in the spring of 1984, phase three of the College of Information Management was the most ambitious of all: an undergraduate program in Information and Records Management. Teaching "core concepts of information management," the program would culminate in a Bachelor of Science in Information and Records Management, would consist of a 60-hour major (the other two-thirds of the course work to be taken in the College of Arts and Sciences and the business school, "thus increasing and supporting the total program of the university," according to the executive officer), and would be "concerned with controlling and retrieving information for others." Graduates would be prepared for such "professional" careers as records managers, data analysts, indexers-abstractors, information brokers, micrographics supervisors, editorial assistants, and information systems trainers. Training in computer programming was not included in the curriculum, for as the executive officer noted,

> ...My own feeling is that the last
> thing I want to teach my people is
> how to program. I think they need
> to have a little bit of understanding
> of what it's all about, but they are
> not programmers, [and] I would
> never send them out of here as pro-
> grammers. They're really in-

formation specialists who see technology as a tool to help match the
information to the user. And we
only need to know a little about
computers to make them work well
and not to be able to pick them
apart, program them, or anything
else. [Computers] are basically
tools....

Systems analysis, information systems design, and database
management, however, figured prominently in the IRM
curriculum. Eventually a Ph.D. program would be added.

Twenty-five entering freshmen was the enrollment
targeted for the fall term of the 1985-85 year. Although a
four-year cycle would be required for administrators to
assess the direction and quality of the program, it was
projected by the 1988-89 academic year a total of 168
undergraduates would be enrolled. The M.A. in Librarianship, the MAIRM, and the certificate programs would
draw an additional 179 students, for a total enrollment in
the CIM, as the College of Information Management was
known, of 347. Four new full-time faculty would be re-
cruited along with three new full-time staff members.

Total direct costs incurred by the CIM, budgeted at
$21,000 for 1984-85, would rise to some $390,000 by
1988-89. An estimated $1.9 million generated by Alpha's
ever rising tuition would offset direct costs for a net
income of $1.6 million by the fifth year. Those pro-
jections, admitted the executive officer, were

very conservative assumptions, especially enrollment target figures.
Enrollment targets are modest since
the university has had considerable

difficulty in the past with target
figures that proved to be too optimistic.

He estimated that by the break-even point in 1986-87,
CIM would be returning to the university roughly $1.44
for each dollar invested, with the caveat that CIM be given

consistent support over the five-year
period and have a full 12-month
program in which to start to market
the new programs.

Four of the benefits of the CIM concept cited by
the executive officer were the following:

1. attracting new students to the
university;

2. increasing the total undergraduate
program of the university and generating more credit hours;

3. attracting the interest of new
donors to a university 'that is un-
dertaking a unique[,] integrated program in information management;
and

4. attracting 'positive national and
international attention to the university' because of the new programs.

Nevertheless, in the words of a former university
administrator, CIM did not have the total support of the
library school faculty: "three or four people [came] into

my office expressing dissatisfaction...criticizing the lack of
leadership of [the executive officer.] Morale was terrible."
Moreover,

> There are a lot of challenges when
> you start stepping on toes. Like
> what do you mean by an un-
> dergraduate program in information
> management? We had over in the
> college of business a very high-
> powered information management
> system.

Perhaps, the former administrator suggested, a "different
type of leadership" on the part of the executive officer
might have "soothed the confrontations that started arising."

The executive officer insists that he "sat down repeatedly" with both the dean and the associate dean of the
business school, and even

> scheduled out areas where we could
> do some team-teaching and cross-
> course swapping in the process of
> things like database management and
> systems analysis.... We were plan-
> ning to do some things, and I think
> there was in some areas a very
> cooperative relationship. I always
> had an excellent relationship with
> [the business school.]

Soon the situation was further aggravated because, as the
executive officer charges,

> The computer science people just
> didn't understand what we were
> trying to do. They think that unless

you are a programmer, you don't
know anything about computers and
how to make them work.

And according to the former administrator,

The [third] part of the political
warfare that started was over here in
our mathematics department; we had
a tremendous growth in computer
technology and size. Now a lot of
this was hardware stuff and a lot of
it was theoretical computer technology, but there were some pretty
high-powered people brought in and
we got all kinds of grants from the
government...on computer technology.

Initially, "[the library school], the school of business and
the computer centers over here in math would start meeting together to see how they could reinforce each other
and help." That, however, was not to be;

...In all honesty, the business school
thought this was strictly a competitive thrust that [the library school]
was trying. Some of the publicity
went out saying that [the library
school] was trying to train people at
the undergraduate level who can
take jobs in industry to handle in-
ventories and information management...working with commercial
products where their people had to
be the source of information gathered all the time and made available

to the business management. Well,
that really raised a lot of hackles
over in the school of business.

Soon it seemed that in many parts of the university hackles
were raised. Of prime concern was the widespread perception that the library school was seeking to boost its
enrollment without a clear or realistic idea of the future
employability of persons who would earn a bachelor's degree in information management.

"I think it could have been handled a lot better,"
observed the former administrator,

if [the executive officer of the library school] had had a little more
skill; ...they really didn't have the
faculty in the library school to move
into this whole new development.
Now they did bring in in the last
couple of years a couple of new
people who had some back-
ground...but they certainly did not
have the status within the university
as being qualified to [teach] what we
call information management.

At issue, then, was a fundamental disagreement and
lack of understanding between and among Alpha's administration, the business school, the departments of computer
science and mathematics, and finally the library school, as
to "what we call information management." And although
he maintains that he had clearly delineated the goals of the
CIM, and had equally clearly defined information management in the process, the executive officer lost a critically
important battle for his turf. He remains convinced that
the CIM concept was unique at Alpha and that it did not

overlap or duplicate courses being offered elsewhere on the campus. "There was plenty of room for cooperative activities here," he remarked, yet

> one of the problems you have in
> higher education is not wanting to
> send your students somewhere else.
> [If] you have 500 credits to gener-
> ate...you don't want to send 300 of
> them to some other department; you
> want to generate your own course
> work so it all counts toward your
> budget and your faculty....So there's
> a reluctance, even in the private
> institution, to send [students] off to
> other departments. We send our
> people all over the place, [but] it was
> less reciprocal [for students from
> other schools and departments com-
> ing over here to the library school
> and taking our courses] than it was
> for our students taking courses in
> other areas.

As the turf battle was being waged, there occurred a second development: Alpha's marketing and recruitment process had broken down. At first the new system, begun by an outside consultant hired by the university in the early 1980s to augment enrollment by means of an elabo-rate marketing campaign, seemed bound for success, even though participation in it was optional. Some of the aca-demic units evidently preferred to do their own marketing without counsel from the centralized enrollment manage-ment staff. Letters of inquiry from prospective students were answered promptly and a number of new promotional materials, described as "slick" by one university official, and designed to attract the attention of sophisticated col-lege-age consumers, were printed at some expense. The li-brary school, which did participate, benefited as well:

according to the executive officer, "the new system worked
so well that [enrollment] went up 16 percent that year."
The next year, however, the consultant was hired as enrollment director; but "when he came on," remarked the
executive officer, "he was not the manager, he was the
consultant. So he spent all this time trying to get other
people to join the system," apparently lacking both authority and full support of the administration. The executive
officer:

> [The enrollment management office]
> lost 900 inquiries of mine between
> December and March. And when
> they found them, most of the
> people--we checked a sample--were
> no longer interested because they
> had deadlines for scholarships and
> everything else. So I raised the
> inquiries for [the library school]
> from 900 to around 2,700 during my
> first few years here, and [enrollment
> management] mis-handled as many
> during a critical time, so that one
> year enrollment increased 16 per-
> cent, and the year after, it went
> down 14 percent.

According to the executive officer, the previously
prompt responses began to lag in mid-autumn, "and by
November [the process of responding to inquiries] was
really falling apart." And although he suspected that letters
from prospective students remained unanswered, he did
not complain until January. He admits that initially he
simply wondered if "there [weren't] just some freak problem." Since the library school was alone among the other
graduate programs that had been using the new marketing
campaign, the executive officer added that "I couldn't
contact other departments." Instead he prepared a report
which he titled "The Failure of the Enrollment Manage-

ment System," which he submitted to the president and
several other of Alpha's administrators. "I didn't make any
accusations," the executive officer continued,

> I just said 'here are the facts, folks:
> you decide whether it's working.'
> Two months later the [enrollment
> consultant] was fired. The problem
> was he was a good friend of [the
> president], and from that time for-
> ward my relationship with [the
> president]...has never been as cordial
> as it was before the time I had to
> assassinate one of his friends.

The executive officer does not believe, however,
that he had enemies in the administration with the possible
exception of the university budget officer who reported to
a vice president. Wryly the executive officer observed,

> I think we [were] doing amazingly
> well in an institution that was trying
> its very best to price itself out of the
> marketplace.

That same vice president disagrees with the executive officer's view that he had no enemies:

> Ninety percent [of those conflicts]
> end up in personality problems be-
> tween administrators...and it's too
> darn bad. [The previous executive
> officer] would have been over here
> talking with [the president] and with
> me and with others. We would all
> be sharing our problems together
> and I never had any of that kind of
> relationship with [the present execu-
> tive officer.] It just is too bad.

When asked to cite specific examples of the executive
officer's alleged shortcomings as an administrator, the vice
president stated that

> what amazed me was that he never
> ...well, most people beat a path to
> your door...he sort of retreated;
> ... he didn't build any bridges.

Yet, admitted the vice president, at the same time the executive officer

> tended to be somewhat confronta-
> tional in his approach...I think in
> many ways his coming precipitated
> what I think began the gradual
> downfall of [the library school.]

By early 1984 the new president had been inau-
gurated, charged by the Board of Trustees to reduce
Alpha's deficit by $2 million at once, and to balance the
budget by 1986. Consultants called in to advise the new
president eventually recommended a bold restructuring of
the university, primarily by sharpening the focus of undergraduate education. An internal review panel, constituted
by the new president, went to work immediately. The
executive officer of the library school was bitter about the
composition of the review panel.

> So we had people from all over the
> institution who knew nothing about
> this program. I wouldn't want to be
> on there with a guy from the physics
> department. That's ridiculous! Why
> should someone from history or
> someplace be evaluating librarian-
> ship? This was a very select group
> and it was not...open and fair and
> democratic.

"It's true," admitted a university official, "there was no librarian" on the review panel.

> What we tried to do was get a fairly
> representative cross-section of the
> undergraduate arts and sciences
> people. There were more of them
> on [the panel] than the others.
> There were two of the graduate
> schools--law and international stud-
> ies. But there were a couple of
> people I wouldn't have appointed.

After meeting day and night at a location some distance from the campus, the review panel called for a sweeping re-evaluation of all 48 of Alpha's academic programs. The process began in March as each unit was requested to provide to the panel what was essentially a statement of self-justification. Noted the president, "issues of fiscal balance and academic programs cannot be considered independently." And according to a vice president,

> What we did was develop a set of
> criteria that we looked at related to
> the centrality, quality, demand, and
> resources of each of [our programs.]
> Each college or school or department
> was given a sort of open-ended
> questionnaire to respond to a whole
> set of issues, to report a response to
> [the review panel.]

The questionnaire sought information on new programs currently underway; a ranking of priorities where teaching, research, and service were concerned; a listing of other M.L.S. programs to which the library school wished to be compared; a display of a 20 percent budget cut as well as a 20 percent increase; a statement about what steps could be taken to improve the program and ways the program is unique and should be retained. "[The library school] did a nice job of filling it out and sending it back," acknowledged the vice president.

Prominent in the library school's response were the indisputable facts that the program had been fully reaccredited in 1980 by the American Library Association and had recently been given a high rating among library schools in a perception study. Teaching, as noted in the response, was said to be the library school's first priority. Second were the maintenance of the program as a "regional center of excellence" in library education and a source of professional expertise in service to the community and the university. Research was ranked third. As the executive officer explained,

> The professional field of library and information science does not, unfortunately, have a variety of places to seek funded research grants.....In addition, much of the research work of a graduate professional school falls into the area of 'applied' scholarly investigation, resulting in dissemination and interpretation of new information to the professional field of concern. However, faculty scholarly activity continues....

Less than three weeks after the review panel had received the library school's response, citing its "thoughtfulness," the panel requested additional information in four areas:

> 1. An explanation for the 13 percent decline in the number of master's degrees granted by the library school over the past three years.

2. An explanation for the 95 percent acceptance rate: what factors
led to the unusually high rate of
accepting applicants? Had the
school's admission policies changed?
How had the acceptance rate
affected student quality?

3. A description of the financial
future of the school, especially in
light of the CIM concept, outlining
measures planned to address the
existing imbalance between revenues
and expenditures.

4. A description of efforts that had
been made to coordinate current and
future programs with the business
school and the departments of
mathematics and computer science.
Would a cooperative venture
strengthen the university's approach
to information management?

In his May 14, 1984, memorandum covering the library school's answers to the review panel's four additional
questions, the executive officer asked that those responses
be read in conjunction with the earlier document in hopes
that the panel "would achieve a full understanding of our
program." The following points paraphrase the May 14
responses.

1. 'The status quo' on the job market has
caused a nationwide decline in the number of
M.L.S. degrees granted by accredited library
schools. Over half the people the library school
accepts but who do not matriculate choose not
to attend Alpha for financial reasons. With the

complete implementation of the CIM concept, the library school would appeal to the 'basic needs of non-library information professionals.'

2. The same admissions criteria have been in effect since 1969. 'A large majority of applicants considered [are] pre-screened.' Based on a personal interview with a faculty member, those who perform well are encouraged to apply. Those who are considered poor academic risks are not denied the right to apply, 'but they are not encouraged.' Mean and median grade point averages of matriculants were displayed demonstrating 'a good indication of a higher caliber of students in the past several years as compared to 8 or 9 years ago.'

3. Recalculated to take into consideration income from two previous summer programs, the ratio of the library school's tuition income to total expense was higher than the .82 shown in the most recent financial analysis, thereby substantially reducing the library school's deficit, variously estimated for 1983 at $144,000 by the university and at much less than that by the library school. 'Revenue enhancement' would result from a stepped-up marketing/recruitment effort; a renewed request for approval of the B.S.I.R.M. degree; an increase in the library school's visibility; greater emphasis on outside grant-seeking over curriculum development which had occupied so much time since 1981; more aggressive fund raising from alumni, corporations, and foundations; appealing to a broader audience by means of cable television and other new technologies that would 'deliver educational experiences' for continuing education and professional development.

4. Naming names and dates of meetings
demonstrated 'significant efforts' that had been
made by the library school administration to
'share information and coordinate program development' with business, mathematics, and
computer science. 'It is not as clear that the
effort has been made by other areas in the university to coordinate with us when they developed programs related to our area....'

And finally, the report noted that the library school had
contributed over $16,000 toward university budget re-
duction in fiscal year 1984 and had committed some
$20,000 for budget reduction in the 1985 fiscal year.
Commented the executive officer, "I never saw twice the
same set of figures they were using in terms of financial
analysis."

On May 17 the executive officer appeared in person before the review panel; he was given one-half hour to
make his case. Still maintaining that he had been autho-
rized to recruit faculty for two positions, the executive
officer went to Dallas for the annual conference of the
American Library Association. That he had been given
permission to recruit is vigorously disputed by a vice
president. On June 11 the review panel made its final
recommendations, and two weeks later the executive officer, in Dallas, was notified of the decision by telephone.
The library school would be closed, along with the theater
department (both found to be "financially exigent" and
irrelevant to the university's mission), the school of
nursing, the undergraduate programs in speech pathology
and education, and the department of anthropology. Although it had been determined to be "comparatively weak,"
the political science department would be retained. And
the executive officer was summoned home.

The objectives of the plan were to revamp Alpha's
organizational structure, to eliminate at least 50 faculty

members, to eliminate or cut back academic programs, and
to refocus the university's mission on undergraduate
education. Said the president, "I did what any good
administrator had to do. I made some decisions about
administrative structure."

The executive officer disagrees. The real reason,
he charges, was

> the institution's mind set. When the
> whole new process started and the
> budget crunch came down on them,
> they realized they had to do some-
> thing to upgrade undergraduate
> education or they were in deeper
> trouble than they ever imagined.
> Undergraduate enrollment is what
> was keeping the institution alive.... I
> think they could have done the
> whole thing without throwing in the
> [program] evaluations. I think the
> program evaluations, frankly, were
> eye-wash to backstop preconceived
> notions of what it is they intended
> to do in the first place.

UNIVERSITY OF BETA

Among library education programs, the University of Beta's was neither venerable nor nationally ranked. Founded in 1945, it was first accredited to grant graduate degrees in 1959. Although in its early years the school had achieved some prominence in school media studies, placing many graduates in school positions throughout the region, by the end of its second decade three-quarters of Beta's M.L.S. graduates went on to their first professional placements in academic, public, and special libraries. "We were the Sears Roebuck of library education," was the way one university official characterized the program.

After the M.L.S. program lost its accreditation in 1983, university administrators made the decision to close the school. Although "difficult," that action was entirely "appropriate," acknowledged a mid-1984 vice-presidential statement to the Board of Trustees, even though the library school

> [had] served so well in a valuable
> role and whose graduates [had] con-
> tributed in many ways and places to
> their profession.

It had been estimated that an expenditure of some $150,000--primarily to increase faculty size and to hire a full-time executive officer--would be required to restore the M.L.S. program to an accreditable state. In the absence, however, of full assurance that the program would be reaccredited even if such an expenditure were made, university officials declined to risk the investment. Said an administrator,

> No, [that's] not a lot of money...[but
> the library school] was one of the
> lowest student/faculty ratio programs
> in the university [7.6:1 for fiscal

> 1982-83] and faculty productivity
> was low. To support those areas that
> are growing, you have to reallo-
> cate.... That's hard for people to
> understand. They keep thinking, 'if
> you really loved me you would let
> this cut pass.'

Letting cuts pass based on emotional attachments was not a
luxury that a public institution which had lost roughly 30
percent of its state support could afford. Moreover, a
noted library educator called upon to assess the library
school's potential for reaccreditation had recommended that
the 1983 judgment by the Committee on Accreditation
(COA) of the American Library Association be left stand-
ing: an appeal should not be filed. Explained an administrator,

> [The consultant] didn't say 'shut it
> down;' but he said 'find out what's
> the problem.' If you're not ac-
> credited you are not a library school
> and so it is unfair and unethical and
> unprofessional to graduate people.
> [Accreditation] is the key, your mark
> of outside sanction.

Thus when its "outside sanction" was withdrawn, administrators maintained that they had no choice but to
eliminate the program.

The M.L.S. represented for those matriculants without previous undergraduate course work a 36-semester
hour commitment, while 30 hours constituted the degree
for students who prior to enrollment had completed at least
nine hours of librarianship courses. Required of all
graduate students were six courses totaling 17 hours. The
customary preparation in academic, public, and special librarianship was available. A Master of Science degree

with specialization in information science was granted as
well. More individualized than the M.L.S. degree, the M.S.
was also promoted as interdisciplinary, with options for
elective study in the departments of mathematics, computer
science, communication, business, and linguistics. Said one
faculty member, despite what he acknowledged as the long
presence of information technology courses in the curriculum,

> It was always like pulling teeth to
> get any kind of electronic equip-
> ment. We finally ended up with a
> fairly strong information science
> program, but it was...a lot of work
> and it need not have been.

A new Master of Library Administration, developed with the business school, was described in the bulletin as a second masters degree for students in "library
related middle management positions;" who seek new
management skills or wish to update their knowledge; or
who "need professional development that can be measured
in dollars and cents." A 30-hour program, the M.L.A.
stipulated 18 hours in information science and management
of technology, six to ten hours from business or related
areas, and an advanced library management seminar. And
finally, the library school offered an undergraduate minor
as part of Beta's B.A. or B.S. degree, either for students
desiring to become teacher/librarian media specialists or
for those planning to enroll in a graduate library science
program after receipt of the undergraduate degree. By the
winter term of 1983, supporting those diverse programs
was a full-time faculty of the library school numbering
five: four assistant professors and one associate professor,
plus a part-time interim executive officer holding the rank
of professor.

Originally the library school was part of the college
of arts and sciences. Credit hours generated by students

enrolled in the various library and information science courses were added into arts and sciences' total. In the 1974-75 academic year the number of hours contributed by the library school amounted to 6201; on-campus course offerings taught by 18 full-time faculty numbered 20; enrollment was 575; and the student/faculty ratio was 18:1. During that period the library school became a separate academic unit. Thus the executive officer, who previously had reported to the dean of arts and sciences, now reported to a vice president.

According to a library school administrator, the move toward autonomy was a result of encouragement from the Committee on Accreditation. She explained;

> There had...been a great tendency on
> the part accreditation requirements
> to try and assist schools to become
> independent in university structures,
> and most of the accreditation visits
> that we had, at one point or another
> during the late 60s and early 70s,
> stressed the fact that the school
> ought to be more independent: that
> [the executive officer] ought to have
> more direct access to the vice presi-
> dent. This school has had a check-
> ered history in that regard anyway.

A faculty member agreed with that assessment but added that the independence for the library school was motivated by a second factor, the ambition of the executive officer.

> She wanted to be a dean and have a
> seat on the administrative council.
> And the only way she could do that
> was to make the [library] school in-
> dependent.

Although her title remained unchanged, she did sit on the administrative council. About not receiving the deanship she commented that the then vice president had told her, "I can't make you a dean because I have all the deans I can fuss with right now." She would have been the only female dean. Moreover, she was the university's affirmative action officer at the time. She now admits that "I really should have fought back on that."

For a time the school's independence as well as its future seemed to be secure. Remarked an administrator,

> [The vice president was] very pro-
> tective; he tended to let [the exec-
> utive officer] do anything she
> wanted to. He was that kind of
> person.

The incumbent vice president, described by one university official as "the granddaddy of the place," eventually re-tired, however, and with his retirement came changes both in reporting relationships and in communication styles. The university official:

> [The new man] already had some 25
> people reporting to him...and when
> the dean of the college of arts and
> sciences that controls half of the
> university departments, most of
> them larger than the library school,
> wanted to see the vice president he
> [saw] the vice president.

It also appeared that the new vice president had little in-terest in the library school, which was soon transferred to a reporting relationship with the associate vice president, who explained the shift by saying,

> Let's face it. When you are going
> through tremendous upheavals in a
> university, and you have huge new
> programs going on, I mean how
> much time can you devote?

To the best recollection of the associate vice president, the
new relationship did not result from a formal restructuring
but because

> I had this tremendous interest in the
> library school. As I viewed it and
> what it needed to do, I saw there
> were great opportunities....[So] I pre-
> pared all of this stuff and went over
> it in a meeting with [the executive
> officer] What are the goals? What
> is the mission for the next two
> years?

He continued,

> [The executive officer] really did not
> think I understood anything about a
> professional program, although I
> [had come] from the college of busi-
> ness, and she also felt that I really
> did not think that library science is
> very close to brain surgery. I mean,
> it is not brain surgery...so what's the
> big deal? Why is it so difficult?

It is the view of another library school administrator that the library school actually lost stature as a result
of its hard-won independence. She noted that

> enrollment was declining even fur-
> ther, and there was a ten-year
> period where [it] dropped tremen-

> dously, and... whenever the statistics
> were printed out for the university
> as a whole--they were done by col-
> leges--it was clear to me that [the
> library school was] in significant
> danger. Enrollment declined, faculty
> declined, and other programs that
> had high enrollment took resources
> away from us.

Those statistics for 1982-83 included 10.8 full-time equivalent faculty (full-time faculty numbered five); total on-
campus enrollment of 273; 1650 credit hours; 20 on-
campus course offerings; and an estimated student/faculty
ratio of 10.8. Contrasted with the 1974-75 statistics, the
new numbers could no longer be ignored, especially in
light of drastic cutbacks in the state university system. At
the same time, however, ambitious new programs in business, computer science, and enginering were initiated and
funded generously. Explained a vice president, "while we
were going to reduction, we were also going to growth.
And when [business, computer science and engineering]
grow, you are growing in other areas," referring to the
interest in mathematics and the pure sciences that is often
a secondary effect of increased enrollment in business and
technical courses. It is widely agreed on the Beta campus
that independence for the library school made it a target
for eventual elimination. The vice president agreed.

> I've always said that. One way to
> protect yourself is just to disappear.
> Get into a larger unit. When all the
> data comes in and here's arts and
> sciences and here's the library
> school, it stands out there all by
> itself. And so you look at it just as
> you look at a major unit. Now, if
> they had been lost in arts and sci-
> ences they would have been just

> another tiny little department...which
> we tend to tolerate because their
> averages are lost.

A matter of more sensitivity but no less significance is the leadership provided by the former executive
officer. A library educator of international prominence,
she was described as a "distinguished, charismatic figure
who was an outstanding faculty leader." "She became
famous in the profession," observed another university
official, but during her tenure as president of a major
professional association--a commitment that lasted for the
better part of three years--in the words of a faculty member, "the school operated without its leader...at the same
time that the university and the library school began to
decline." It has been said that a strong and authoritative
management style made it difficult for her to delegate to
others. Although when professional responsibilities demanded her attentions elsewhere and she did name an acting executive officer, there is widespread sentiment that
she never relinquished control. It would appear that the
acting executive officer, while given great deal of responsibility for managing the school, had minimal authority to
function independently in the incumbent's absence.

The acting executive officer during those years
maintains that she tried to compensate by involving the
faculty more deeply in decision making.

> I was extremely active with the fac-
> ulty and tried to make up for the
> gap in administrative leadership. We
> had lots of committees and things
> like this to compensate, but the only
> problem was we couldn't compensate
> at the very level needed, which was
> in the vice president's office.

A vice president:

> Well, she delegated a lot but she was
> gone. Now that happens a lot in
> other programs; people aren't saying
> she was gone all the time. The
> president is gone a lot...I mean, the
> place doesn't collapse.

A faculty member expressed bitterness about what he
termed the executive officer's "neglect" of the school.
"Nobody benefited from her being gone." And when she
announced her retirement, the faculty member noted,

> She didn't assure an orderly transfer
> of power. Plus she didn't get out.
> She stepped down but she stayed
> around. [Her] presence was there,
> which is of course not the way to
> go.

She has admitted that perhaps she did stay around
too long, although at no time did she believe that her
presence impeded the search for her replacement. "It was
a faculty search committee, and I was not allowed any in-
put," she remarked.

> I guess I am terribly negative about
> that committee. I was concerned
> about the chair, and I was concerned
> about the way they went about it,
> and I was disturbed because at that
> point they were saying they didn't
> want a woman director. Now that
> hurt in a way.

She even suspects that a lettter expressing interest in the
position, written to the search committee by a well-known
female library educator, was never answered. Although

the executive officer had given two years' notice prior to her retirement, the search for her replacement was arduous and long. She portrayed the three final candidates as "just inadequate for the particular situation." Indeed, she noted, "the faculty--all the faculty--and the administration turned them down point blank."

A vice president confirmed that

> the amazing thing about it is that it
> was an embarrassment. They
> brought in people from unaccredited
> schools. That was probably the
> beginning of the end. Anyway, we
> went over the names of the people
> in the [library school] who could be
> the acting [executive officer.] I'll
> tell you, it was slim.

One by one members of the faculty were approached. "We were pushed out on a limb," remembered the executive officer. Finally a faculty member agreed to the appointment until a permanent executive officer could be found. "He was chosen by default," she said: "we were desperate." And, she observed,

> I hate to say it, because the [faculty
> member chosen] is an awfully nice
> guy, but I do think that if there had
> been a person who had been able to
> make decisions back then, we would
> not have been closed.

In February of 1981 the program received conditional accreditation from the American Library Association. The review contained 27 recommendations which were to be met during the ensuing two-year period. Major concerns are paraphrased as follows.

1. <u>Goals and objectives</u>. Those should be more widely disseminated and more precisely define the constituency of the school. The faculty should review the effects of other program elements (undergraduate, specialist, specializations, joint degrees, and off-campus instruction) on the M.L.S.

2. <u>Curriculum</u>. A long-range plan should be developed. A policy should be determined for exemptions from core course requirements and consistently appplied. Steps should be taken to assure the quality and parity of the M.L.S. program as taught on the main campus and at extensions.

3. <u>Faculty</u>. Numbers and strengths should be reviewed in light of curricular priorities. Part-time faculty should be equal in quality to full-time faculty. Scholarly productivity should be increased by all faculty members. Teaching loads should be considered for reduction when faculty present valid proposals for scholarly projects. Future recruiting should aim for a better balance of minority representation.

4. <u>Students</u>. Sound recruitment procedures should be developed, especially for minority students. Admissions requirements should be aligned more realistically with academic requirements. Alumni should be regularly surveyed regarding curricular decisions.

5. <u>Governance</u>. A permanent chief administrator should be selected immediately. Questions about the school's place in the university should be resolved. The number of committees should be decreased. The budget allocations for travel, operating expenses, and the laboratory

library should be reviewed. A stable size for
the faculty should be determined after consul-
tation with university administrators.

6. Physical Resources and Facilities. Better
faculty office space should be found.
Resources available at off-campus instruction
sites should be reviewed for adequacy. The
future of the laboratory library and its librarian
should be resolved.

Yet, according to the retired executive officer, the
library school "fussed around" and did little to begin to
deal with the recommendations until the following May.
"We didn't do anything," a faculty member admitted.

At the same time the university was engaged in a
sweeping program re-evaluation. Each program would be
given a priority rating from 1 to 4. Those ratings would
provide direction for reallocation of what were then extremely scarce resources. They included the following:

1. increase resources;
2. maintain existing resources;
3. decrease resources and/or merge with
   other programs to decrease total
   commitment of resources; and
4. phase out.

The review delivered a second blow to the library school:
it was given a priority 4, or to be phased out. No one in
Beta's administration, however, was able to provide any
documentary evidence to explain how or why the priority
4 was assigned. In the words of one administrator, "a
massive appeal" then ensued; the priority 4 was subsequently revised to a 3. According to that administrator,
though, while the news about the priority 4 was widely

disseminated on the campus and throughout the library education community, the result of the appeal was not; and enrollment continued to decline.

The interim executive officer was removed. His replacement met with COA the following summer: on her agenda was a request of the membership to consider the effects of planned curriculum revision on the M.L.S. program's accreditation status. COA requested a second self-study. Meeting again with COA in the winter of 1983, the interim executive officer was "surprised" to receive 39 additional questions from the Committee, an action that necessitated a supplement to the second self-study. A second site-visit team arrived on the campus in March of 1983 and in due time issued its recommendations. Among those were the following, again paraphrased:

> 1. <u>Goals and Objectives</u>. They should clearly delineate between the goals and objectives for the M.L.S. program and other programs of the school. They should clearly relate to all constituencies served and analyze the impact of the M.L.S. on other programs.
>
> 2. <u>Curriculum</u>. In planning for a revision, the school should analyze the extent of available resources to ensure that it is prepared to provide the program as announced.
>
> 3. <u>Faculty</u>. Scholarly productivity should be increased both in amount and in quality. A vacant position should be filled so that coverage of the goals and objectives of the M.L.S. degree program are met. The school should evaluate the total

number of faculty required to support its goals and objectives.
Procedures for peer review, promotion, and tenure decisions should be made consistent with those for other teaching faculty of the university.

4. Students. Recruiting should be evaluated and application of admissions requirements should be consistent with stated policy. Exceptions should be clearly recorded.

5. Governance. The school's anomalous position in the university structure was recognized. The faculty should play a greater role in decisions that determine the future of the school. A permanent executive officer should be appointed as soon as possible. Support staff size should be increased.

The Committee on Accreditation voted on June 25, 1983, to discontinue the accreditation of the program leading to the M.L.S. degree at the University of Beta. The retired executive officer is still bitter. Of prime concern to her was the composition of the site-visit team, two members of which she described as "anything but sympathetic" to a terminal masters degree program at a regional institution. A faculty member provided a longer reply.

COA leaves a lot to be desired.... I think there is a certain kind of library school that always gets accredited. [COA] will never disaccredit Illinois; they will never disaccredit Michigan.... I consider the process archaic. I [think] the

> standards need to be radically re-
> worked.... ALA or COA has always
> operated on the assumption that if
> they came in and gave you proba-
> tionary or pulled your ticket, that
> was enough to scare the local admin-
> istration into spending a lot of
> money [to] rectify whatever was
> wrong. It didn't happen here.

He claimed that "COA didn't understand austerity: what they said was in diametric opposition to the philosophy of the administration, which was 'cut, cut, cut.'"

> The former executive officer also maintained that the site visit team was "turned off" by the then academic vice president. In fact, she said, one of the members of the team confided to her that "you have the most awful administration I have ever run into." Between March when the team visited the campus and June when the disaccred-itation decision was made, that vice president was fired; yet, noted the interim executive officer,

> COA's rules indicate that they base
> all decisions on factors which are in
> existence at the time of the visit.
> Therefore, the change in vice presi-
> dents, the [new] tenure of a staff
> member, the work on filling the key
> appointment, and an increase in the
> operating budget were apparently
> ignored.

> As is customary, Beta was given six weeks to file an appeal. A well-respected library educator was con-sulted. In a thoughtful piece of writing that provides remarkable insight into the workings of the accreditation (and disaccreditation) process, the consultant advised Beta

not to appeal; because, he wrote, appeal is advisable only
if evidence of one or more of three issues can be found.

> 1. Whether the visiting team conducted itself
> properly during the four-day [site visit] period
> in accordance with rules set forth in the Manual
> [of instructions for COA site-visit teams];
>
> 2. Whether the team determined the facts cor-
> rectly as expressed in its factual section of the
> report; and
>
> 3. Whether the team, and the COA itself, then
> properly interpreted the standards in relation-
> ship to those facts.

Moreover, he concluded that in all likelihood the members
of the team and the Committee on Accreditation believed
the final decision to be "incontestable;" and he advised
against an appeal.

The former executive officer:

> I really think the university should
> have grieved, even though they were
> advised not to by a very prestigious
> [library educator.] Of course I have
> been angry with COA for a good
> many years--long before we got
> disaccredited because I think they
> have not moved with the times.

As a result of the decision, current students would
be given 18 months in which to complete their programs
without losing the recognition of an accredited professional
degree. The executive officer wrote,

> Equity and protection within the
> university, especially as provided in

the past year or so, can not erase the
problems which have developed over
several years. Regardless, the school
has been a credit to this institution
and serious consideration must be
given to the ramifications of closing
it.

The equity and protection to which she referred apparently
was a vice president's almost single-handed crusade to
keep the school afloat. The former executive officer
commented that "[the vice president] didn't believe it; he
thought he had saved the school." However his efforts
came too late, she believes, to have had any meaningful
effect.

That vice president, meanwhile, had put together a
report outlining four options to be considered. He dismissed as unlikely the possibility of an appeal to COA,
especially in light of the consultant's recommendation.
The university could seek accreditation in two more years
following the expenditure of $150,000; yet he wrote,

This does not seem a wise expenditure of dollars in a program among
the lowest in student/faculty.ratio
and not high in faculty productivity.
Moreover, there is no certainty that
we would gain accreditation, and a
recent trend in library education indicates a strong tendency not to accredit programs with fewer than ten
faculty.

A third possibility, to continue offering an unaccredited
program, he dismissed as "unrealistic," as decline almost
surely would accelerate; and resources devoted to the pro-

gram could be used with greater advantage elsewhere in the university. Therefore, he concluded, phasing out the school was the fourth and only option.

Thus at the June 15, 1984, meeting of the Board of Trustees, the library school at the University of Beta was officially closed as of May 1 of the following year. Said the retired executive officer:

> I maintain that if they had waited
> one year, they wouldn't have had to
> close the school. It was a question
> of poor timing. And the thing that
> really made me angry--after they
> had done that and said they had
> done it to save $100,000 [sic]--they
> did a blacktop job out in front of
> the university parking lot that
> probably cost about that amount of
> money.

GAMMA UNIVERSITY

At Gamma University library education had enjoyed a tradition of solid respectability. Announcing the establishment of the library school in 1928, a news item hailed librarianship as an attractive career choice, for "...the library is now an opportunity, not a rest cure or a pensioned sinecure." Students would be prepared for the "several types of library work now demanded throughout the state." Graduates of the library school's M.L.S. program typically met with success when they sought professional employment, especially as the university's urban environment grew in population and became an important regional center for high technology, commerce, and finance.

Citing in August of 1981 a budgetary shortfall of some $25 million, Gamma's president included closing the library school in a scenario that illustrated how dramatic expense-cutting might have to be. The president's words proved to be prophetic: several months later the university's governing board approved paring $15 million from Gamma's $329 million operating budget, and one of the programs determined to be superfluous to the university's mission was indeed the library school. Admission of new students would be suspended indefinitely as of the 1982 summer term. Said a university official,

> We requested planning documents
> from five or six departments. This
> is a land-grant institution, but you
> can't do everything. We are the
> largest single campus in the world; I
> guess at least in the United States.
> In the enormity of this enter-
> prise....one would think you could
> wring out some things, [but the uni-
> versity] really didn't have to respond

> to everything that the community or
> the legislature and society asked [it]
> to do.

"You can't do everything," he explained; "it became 'what
can we pick off?'" Picked off, along with masters, specialist, and doctoral programs of the library school, were
South Asian studies, undergraduate pharmacy and metal-
lurgy programs, and on a satellite campus home economics,
the geography department, and the masters program in
history. Targeted for reduction on the main campus were
agricultural engineering, dental hygiene, physical education, educational administration, Afro-American and
African studies, industrial relations, East Asian studies,
and physical chemistry. At regional campuses ten additional programs would be reduced. Tenured faculty whose
jobs would be affected by the cuts and reductions would
be given several options from which to choose, including
early or phased retirement and transfers to other units
within the university.

Commented a former library school faculty
member,

> It sort of reminded me of Russian
> Roulette in a way. At the end of a
> budget period with the retrenchment
> they were pooling money and every-
> body--it was sort of like a piranha
> pool--would sit around the table and
> they had all their requests and this
> gave tremendous power to the
> administration. 'Now, no one's
> going to get everything they want;
> probably most of you aren't going
> to'...it's not good budgeting; it's not
> good logic. It creates a ravenous

> kind of appetite. [The admin-
> istration] wanted us to become
> another MIT.

Fifty-four quarter hours of graduate study were
required, including a minimum of 37 credits in library
science, a minimum of eight credits in related fields, and a
research project of at least four credits. The remaining
five credits could be taken in the library school or a
related field, or to extend the research requirement. Four
courses--foundations of library and information services,
reference, organization of information, and applications of
information science and technology--comprised the curricular core. According to the bulletin, the option of
taking as much as one-fourth of their total credits outside
the library school permitted students

> to increase their knowledge in a
> traditional discipline or to explore
> in some depth the contribution to
> library science of such fields as
> business administration, management
> information systems, computer
> science, archives, speech
> communication, [and] adult educa-
> tion.

A thesis could substitute for the research project if students so desired. Such exposure to other schools and departments brought library school students into close contact
with outside faculty who served variously as program
advisors and research directors.

Many students came to Gamma for its specialty in
health sciences librarianship, the completion of which
could lead at that time to certification by the Medical
Library Association. Traineeships at a local Veterans

Administration hospital provided an opportunity for students to gain practical experience in that area while enrolled in the masters program.

Matriculating students already licensed as teachers in the state could obtain certification in school librarianship upon completion of 26 credits of library school course work, and a media generalist certificate was available to students who completed 42 credits. Both of those programs were offered cooperatively by the library school and the school of education. Experienced librarians could earn a specialist certificate, awarded upon completion of 44 credits beyond the masters degree. Highly individualized, the specialist program was designed to appeal to persons with at least two years of prior professional experience.

Described as cross-disciplinary in nature, the Doctor of Philosophy provided an opportunity for students "to develop indepth knowledge of librarianship and to pursue research aimed at producing an original contribution to the body of knowledge of the field." A former faculty member commented, however, that by the early 1980s, only "a handful of people" pursued the Ph.D. in librarianship at Gamma. One reason for the low enrollment, he said, was a dearth of funding earmarked for the support of full-time doctoral study.

The masters program was once again fully reaccredited in 1981, and the report produced by the visiting team representing the American Library Association's Committee on Accreditation listed the following as special strengths of Gamma University's M.A. program. Those are paraphrased below.

> 1. The goals and objectives are 'clearly defined and articulated,' demonstrating on the part of the school 'a strong awareness of interdisciplinary study.'

2. The curriculum is a 'carefully constructed program' based on the goals and objectives presenting a 'unified whole.'

3. The school has a 'corps of full-time faculty who are well-qualified to function in the graduate faculty' of the university.

4. Research productivity is 'good.'

5. Student guidance and advisement are 'quite remarkable.'

It would appear, then, that quality--at least as determined by the American Library Association's 1972 *Standards* for Accreditation and interpreted by the 1980 visiting team-- was not an issue in the closing of Gamma's library school.

Pointing to possible causes of the school's demise, however, a university academic administrator observed that the library school presented a "dichotomy," remarking that

there wasn't any problem in the
number of students; there wasn't any
problem in placement [of graduates];
but there was a disjuncture between
the curriculum and placements.
There was a big shift being made in
librarian positions in [the area.]
People needed training in this new
technology....

The library school fulfilled its mission, he continued, only "in the sense that its graduates somehow found jobs....If you measure [quality] by [the library school's] product and placements they should have felt safe." Fundamentally, however, "you have to go back about ten years" to understand why the school was closed." Limited retrenchment-- in the form of program evaluation in response to dwindling funds and a changing student population--first began at Gamma in the mid-1970s. As part of its examination of some of the university's academic programs, the administration commissioned two reviews of the library school.

Results of the first, made by an external committee composed of three well-known library educators, were reported in May of 1975. Paraphrased from the external review are the following:

>   1. It is 'entirely appropriate' that Gamma maintain a quality library science program. Both masters and advanced-level programs should be continued and strengthened.

>   2. Research is an essential mission of a graduate library school at a 'great university such as [Gamma.'] 'If such contribution to knowledge is not done here, it will likely not be done.'

>   3. The only accredited library school in the state, especially one connected with a state-supported institution, bears heavy responsibility [for research], and [that] mission needs...to be emphasized by the library school.

>   4. Regarding its mission of research and contribution to knowledge, the library school's output is very weak. 'Very few of the faculty have had recent publications, and almost none have significant ongoing research or scholarly projects underway.'

>   5. Weaknesses in the school's research output can be attributed to weaknesses in its resources and support.

>   6. The curriculum, although well-planned, lacks 'variety and depth.' Local adjunct faculty

should be utilized more extensively for specialized courses as should doctoral students as teachers of the core curriculum.

The external review committee concluded that while the library school "has many strengths," it is "greatly underfunded," and it urged the library school faculty and the university administration to "work together to arrive at priorities in goals and objectives and strategies for developing the resources to accomplish them." And finally, the school "will need the moral support and the quality control" of [the university] in "making tough decisions that will undoubtedly be necessary in remaining true to its missions." Half a decade later the principals involved were still engaged in making tough decisions and garnering moral support.

At the same time the external reviewers were making their report public, an internal team appointed by the university's Social Sciences Policy and Review Committee was also reporting its evaluation of the library school. Members of the six-person panel included faculty from the departments of psychology, history, the library school, and the school of journalism as well as two students--one from the library school and one representing speech communication. Perhaps even more critical than the external review, the internal panel's report noted, among other things, that

1. Ongoing research is 'not visible in current and impressive depth.'

2. Significant research productivity is necessary.

3. The thrust of the program of the library school is 'out of balance and must be shifted toward deeper commitments and the advancement of knowledge.'

4. Members of the panel were 'struck with the toll retrenchment has taken on the morale of the staff.'

5. Although the faculty feel 'at home' in the college of arts and sciences, committee members acknowledged that 'professional schools have special needs which require unique patterns of funding, staffing, and administration.' Questioning whether arts and sciences had 'adequate resources at its disposal,' the panel advised that a move out of arts and sciences might be necessary if the program 'cannot be adequately supported to accomplish its goals...within the present administrative structure.'

6. The budget is below 'any kind of reasonable operating level,' and audio-visual and computer access are 'all but non-existent in a school which sees the importance of electronic technology in the communication of information.'

In a written response to those reviews an unsigned memorandum typed on library school letterhead indicated, somewhat surprisingly, that

> we are grateful to both committees
> for their review of our programs.
> With one or two exceptions, we find
> the results both objective and sym-
> pathetic, with a serious orientation
> toward improving our programs.

The two reports evidently did not escape the attention of those administrators who had commissioned them. Said one official,

> They were almost being told 'shape
> up or ship out' ten years ago. [My

> predecessor] pointed out what he
> thought was the decline and the
> erosion of the...school. It was really
> a struggle to get the full library
> school faculty behind...changes....

About the apparently unanimous sentiment that the library
school suffered from chronic underfunding and was a
perennial loser in the university budgeting and resource
allocation process, he remembered,

> The low ratings were done by fac-
> ulty committees....There had to be
> programmatic planning documents
> saying where you were going, why
> you were doing this and why this
> was a priority, etc. And the Budget
> Advisory Committee inevitably came
> up with the lowest ratings for the
> requests from the library school.

When asked to speculate as to why the library school's
ratings were so low, the administrator replied that

> the library school had become iso-
> lated...and [was] not participating.
> People didn't know them in a social
> way. They knew them in a scholarly
> way, but as being out of date. But
> there was something more here that
> was more than tiredness; there was
> dead wood in the sense of not being
> interested in the way the world was
> changing.

He also recalled that

> we wrote a report saying that the
> library school is not up to quality.

> [The then executive officer] and a
> few people came over and wanted
> me to explain that. After I ex-
> plained it, they left. They didn't
> oppose it. It was not like getting rid
> of economics or English; in fact, it
> was an easy task. It was...like the
> arguments over veterinary medicine.
> How many veterinary medicine
> graduate programs do you need in
> the country?

Former faculty members expressed bitterness in
their perception that the then executive officer did not, as
one described it, "stand up and fight for the school."

> The library school had had...a strong
> administration to begin with. [The
> executive officer until the late
> 1960s] was really the last of the old-
> boy network. [The library school]
> was run on the golf course....The
> faculty then became loaded with
> [tenured] people who simply did not
> have the qualifications and no in-
> tention of getting them, and [the
> school] became a dumping ground
> for tired administrators. [The exec-
> utive officer who succeeded him]
> had no idea as to where we were go-
> ing....Maintaining the status quo was
> his goal...no vision at all. [He] was
> never willing to do more. He would
> say, 'well, if we do that we're just
> going to have to ask for more
> money'....And he wouldn't do it. He
> kept a low profile...so low that [the
> administration] finally stomped on
> us. He thought he was dealing with

> people in the administration who
> were gentlemen and scholars; and
> they weren't.

And another former faculty member recalled that

> [the executive officer] definitely
> wanted the position. I would say
> that [his] first term probably went
> pretty well; it was a holding situa-
> tion. There was nothing really new.
> [He] is brilliant; there was no ques-
> tion about it. But his basic stance
> was 'wait and see.' He offended no
> one. He didn't please anyone either,
> but he didn't offend anyone. The
> program was definitely at a stand-
> still.

Unfortunately the executive officer declined to be interviewed for this study.

It would appear, then, that during the most critical
period in the rapidly ending life of the library school, as
retrenchment moves threatened and faculty morale declined, it became virtually defenseless in the eyes of
university administrators. The review panels' recommendations that the interests of the library school might be
better served by a move out of the college of arts and
sciences--toward independence, although no one in authority apparently ever proposed complete independence
for the school--was never considered further. Faculty
members vigorously deny any part in the school's decline.
As late as the autumn of 1981, said one,

> We would tell [the executive officer],
> 'we need more faculty; ask for more
> faculty.' And we assumed that when
> the faculty took a vote, in the colle-

> gial pattern [the executive officer
> would ask for more faculty.] [But]
> he had gone to the administration
> with a totally different story; he was
> telling them 'no, we don't need more
> faculty or whatever....We'll go along
> with you, whatever you want.' He
> wanted to keep in their good graces.
> It went then from that point on
> downhill.

Concerning the repeated charge that their research productivity was inadequate, several former faculty commented that time spent on student advising and professional responsibilities precluded research, even though one of the 1975 reviews described the faculty's overall professional service as "less than the profession (in the state particularly) has a right to expect." It should be noted that productivity did rise in the late 1970s as a result of two new faculty appointments, yet it became increasingly apparent that the 1975 reviews were not to be forgotten.

Shortly after Gamma's president made his 1981 public announcement of the $25 million deficit, suggesting austerity measures that might include closing the library school, the university's chief academic officer wrote a long and thoughtful letter, given wide distribution throughout the university system and in the media, which boldly outlined the criteria that would be used in upcoming retrenchment-related program reviews. Those factors that would assist university officials in "reaching judgments on program priorities," the vice president wrote, "can be interpreted only within the context of the mission of the university:

> It is the premier academic institution
> in the State and a national resource,
> responsible as a land-grant institu-
> tion for using its capacity to respond

>to the economic, social, and cultural
>needs of the State and nation, and
>committed to teaching, research, and
>service,...it was agreed that at least
>the following factors would have to
>be weighed in determining program
>priority....

He enumerated five criteria; too extensive in the original
for full reporting, paraphrased excerpts appear below.

>Quality. ...It is difficult, as a practical matter,
>to build quality in a conscious and deliberate
>way...Once a University has achieved a high
>level of quality in a program, it should make
>every effort to preserve it; and where an ob-
>vious opportunity exists to make a substantial
>improvement in quality with a realistic in-
>vestment of resources, it should be taken.

>Connectedness. ...The extent to which the pro-
>grams of a department or college serve other
>departments and colleges.

>Integration. The University's particular com-
>mitment to teaching, research, and service sug-
>gests that those programs that integrate all of
>those activities well are especially appropriate
>and important.

>Uniqueness. ...Where it has a unique and useful
>program, [the university] should have a strong
>commitment to maintain it. However, in mak-
>ing this determination, it is also important to
>consider whether the program is appropriate to
>the University's role and strengths, and whether
>it could or should be offered elsewhere.

<u>Demand</u>. Demand is obviously an important
factor, but we must be careful not to interpret
it too narrowly. That is, we must avoid con-
sidering demand to be measured only by the
number of students seeking admission to regular, full-time undergraduate or graduate programs.

And the vice president concluded by acknowledging that

there is no easy or agreed-upon way
of weighing those factors and we
have made no attempt to place them
in any rigid order of priority.
However, each program can be assessed in terms of each of the factors and, even though that will not
lead to precise priority order for all
programs, we expect to be able to
identify those few programs that rate
very high in almost all categories
and those that rate relatively low.

"It was," as one former library school faculty member
wryly observed, "as though they'd already decided to kill
the library school and made up the standards to be sure
we'd be unable to meet them."

     In due course the library school was asked to pre-
pare a statement of self-justification to be presented to the
newly-formed Budget Advisory Committee, a crisis-man-
agement team constituted from within the school of arts
and sciences, at a meeting scheduled for December 20,
1981. That statement provided in only the most general
way descriptive data concerning the school's mission;
demand for its programs (expressed largely in terms of
credit hours generated); a selective list of faculty research
and service (although no persons were named and details

were sketchy at best); and quality of the program (the 1981 COA reaccreditation report was heavily quoted.)

Following the December meeting, the Budget Advisory Committee requested of the library school a second document. Even its title, "The Library School and the College of Liberal Arts," is revealing, for it suggests that the committee had begun to scrutinize the library school's place in, and salience to, the mission of the college in which it uneasily resided. More sharply focused and better detailed than its predecessor, that report dated January 5, 1982, consisted of four parts: Uniqueness and Relation to the College Mission Statement; The Curriculum and the Market; Faculty Service and Recognition; Library Education in the [geographic region]; and an appendix, which contained portions of the 1981 reaccreditation report.

On April 10, the Budget Advisory Committee met to consider "the priority of the Library School in comparison with the other programs of the University and to develop a set of recommendations" to be made regarding the future of the school. Having heard previous testimony of library school officials and having read both of the documents, the committee summarized its recommendations in a three-page report dated April 30 and titled "Report on Library School Hearing." The news was not good. In a section of the report subheaded "Supporting Information," the following points were made and are paraphrased here.

> While the library school has the only accredited program in the state, two unaccredited programs exist, and neighboring states to the east and south also have accredited programs.

> The number of M.A. degrees has declined, on the average, 26 percent over the past five years and 'appears to be indicative of a trend.'

No Ph.D.'s have been awarded by the library school in the past three years, and only three have been granted in the past six years.

There are no 'active, externally supported research grants' in the school. Only one grant proposal has been submitted to an external agency in the past four years, although a faculty member received a Fulbright lectureship.

It would appear that 'significant changes' would be necessary to correct 'observed deficiencies.' In the absence of increases in support for the university as a whole, 'these changes would require collaboration between the Library School faculty and faculty in other departments, possibly external support and certainly a commitment by the School's faculty to these changes.'

While such changes have been discussed with representatives of the library school 'over the past month and a half, but as yet no formal or informal contacts have been made by the Library School faculty with other departments with which they might interact and there appears to be no consensus in the faculty to pursue these changes.'

And finally,

'It does not appear that the programs as presently constituted can continue to be supported in preference to programs that are more highly connected to other University programs or that exhibit a more thorough integration of teaching, research, and service. While the School does serve a need, demand appears to be dropping, and more importantly, the programs

are not responding to that need in a manner
consistent with the academic leadership appropriate to a leading research University.'

The committee recommended that admissions be
suspended indefinitely with the summer term of 1982; that
courses necessary for completion of the masters degree be
continued for three years so that currently enrolled students could finish the degree; and that a task force be
formed to examine during the next year the feasibility of
developing a restructured program that would "provide opportunities for curricular and research activities in information processing and management as well as in the more
classical aspects of librarianship." "If and when," the
recommendations concluded, "the restructured program is
approved by [the university's governing board] upon the
recommendation of the President, the admission of students
can be resumed."

News items pick up the story from that point.
"Library School is safe, for now," announced an article
published in the campus newspaper on July 14, 1982: a
newly-appointed executive officer, given 18 months to
preside over an examination of whether a new program
could be designed and implemented, had signed a three-
year contract to "carry on" the existing program until all
matriculated students could complete the M.L.S. Six
months later another campus headline reported that a
"Committee seeks to revitalize gasping Library School:"

The school's last chance rests in the
hands of a committee that will begin
a final review of the school this
month. But if the school survives, it
will almost certainly take on a different shape. The committee's job
will be to find ways to bring the
program up to date so that it reflects
recent developments in library sci-

ence. Then the committee will have
to decide whether the University
should put the money and effort into
rebuilding it.

"There are some obvious areas of overlap between...
computer science, records management, human services,
and library science," the new executive officer acknowledged in the article, "but no one knows where it's
heading." Several others agreed that a relationship between
computer science and the library school could "be a leading
program moving [the library school] into this information
society," although a member of the task force warned that
"if the University is going to have a library science
program, it should be on the cutting edge of current
research."

It is possible that in different circumstances the
leadership of the new executive officer, in concert with
the moral support of other departments in the university
and an infusion of funds with which to modernize facilities and hire new faculty, might have been sufficient to
fashion a new information management program at Gamma
University. That, however, was not to be, despite a great
deal of time and effort expended by a number of individ-
uals--the executive officer, the local task force, and outside consultants alike. One university official described
the results of the task force's work as "an abortion." "We
couldn't restructure it," he noted; "we had to kill it. And
quietly we closed the school." Sadly he observed that

everybody tells me privately, 'yeah,
that was the right decision.' It's like
laying Grandma away and you expect her to die, and she does and
nobody thinks about it after that.
It's just natural. I guess that was the
most disappointing yet [confirming]

thing about the earlier reviews.
There was nothing within that faculty that was going to save it.

And a former faculty member said wistfully,

It was a nice sort of program; it
wasn't really hurting anybody, but it
became dispensable....

UNIVERSITY OF DELTA

In 1903 when Andrew Carnegie settled $100,000 in United States Steel Corporation bonds upon the University of Delta for the establishment of a library school, it became the seventh such program in America to be affiliated with an institution of higher learning, opening its doors in the fall of 1904 to 14 students. Many years later its executive officer boasted that with the possible exception of the medical school, the library school had done more than any other unit of the university to spread Delta's reputation "both nationally and beyond the seven seas." That same administrator still later would predict a time of reckoning for library education at Delta and elsewhere, noting that in the modern university the educational preparation of librarians had come to occupy a position "low on the academic totem pole."

Following the January 1984 suspension of admissions and a recommendation by the university's academic vice president that library education at Delta be phased out, rumors of the impending closing began to circulate, sending shock waves throughout the library education community. "If [Delta] were having that kind of trouble," one library educator remarked, "it meant that no one was safe." It was not, however, until more than a year later-- an interval of extraordinary bitterness and anger, false hopes and disappointment during which the library school existed in a type of academic receivership administered by the vice president's office--that the executive committee of the Board of Trustees voted to close the school. "Library school's last chapter is the ledger," proclaimed a newspaper headline.

"The proximate cause," the academic vice president wrote,

> for seeking closure of the school is
> the state of financial exigency in
> which the school found itself

> ...However...its financial deficit
> [estimated at $1.3 million over an
> accumulated five-year period] was
> symptomatic of serious underlying
> pathologies.

Some of the "pathologies" he claimed included limited job opportunities for librarians, the poor quality of students enrolled in the M.L.S. program, and a dearth of leadership in library education which had caused a search committee to abandon a lengthy quest for a new executive officer. Those issues and others were to figure prominently in the Trustees' decision to close the school and the events which preceeded it.

> Said a vice president:

> [Phasing out a program] is not
> something you want to do. I mean,
> here's this nice little school; and I
> would bet that 50 percent of [the
> academic vice president's]' and my
> time for two years was spent think-
> ing about the future of eight faculty
> members and 50 students....Nobody
> likes to close a school down. You
> spend a lot of your chips on some-
> thing like that.

The academic vice president agreed.

> Yes, it was two years out of our
> lives. It was a tough two years, but
> it was turnaroundable almost at any
> point; eminently turnaroundable.
> The situation was chronic but so was
> Chrysler's.

What might have made the difference, he commented, was
a strong leader. "This university operates on a strong dean
model, and if you don't have one, you're in the bag: I
couldn't find one." A vice president remembered,

> We were prepared to go out there
> with our checkbooks and hire some
> talent away from somewhere,...[but]
> the best people don't just move for
> money. The situation...was not very
> tempting to somebody who really
> was on the rise.

It is sad and ironic, in view of Delta's reputed
prestige as "the mother of library school deans," as one
administrator expressed it, that as the course of its own
future was being determined by others, university officials
were unable to find a candidate for the position of executive officer who was acceptable to them.

Students came to Delta in pursuit of the M.L.S.
from many states and over 40 foreign countries. Due to its
pioneering efforts in teaching computerized information
storage and retrieval, the library school had been widely
regarded for its innovative practices in library and information science education. According to the bulletin, the
school "stressed program development in information science while retaining the commitment to the development
of the state of the art of librarianship through its library
education programs. "Of course we need children's librarians," a faculty member admitted, "but I'm not sure we
should have been teaching them here." The school's mission statement emphasized advancing the "accessibility,
communication, and use of recorded knowledge and information resources in society through educational, research,
and professional activities;" and the curriculum had recently been revised to allow graduates "a relatively high
degree of mobility among library and information functions within diverse settings." Delta's Ph.D. program,

established in 1956, was notably interdisciplinary, with the
major part of course work carried by other departments in
the university. It focused, according to the bulletin, on
"investigations into significant problems in knowledge
communications and information transfer," and the degree
was awarded in recognition of "significant academic
achievement...that represents a substantive contribution to
existing knowledge" in those two areas. By the early 1980s
enrollment in the doctoral program had dwindled to approximately 15 students. "We never took more than five or
six [applicants] a year," explained an administrator,
"because of advising responsibilities." She continued,

> But I think we reached the point
> where we [were admitting applicants]
> because they helped carry the mas-
> ters program. A lot of the Ph.D.s
> we granted were really wasted
> degrees.

Thirty-six hours constituted the M.L.S. degree,
providing competencies in either "specialization of applications in a given library or information environment"
or "the in-depth study of a given library or information
function applicable to a variety of conditions." The curriculum was composed of six major areas: information
area, which included information sources and organization
of information; management area; technology area; an information science specialty program; a library science specialty program; and general electives. It was said to be
"desirable" for matriculating students to have mastered
basic computer skills and to demonstrate some knowledge
of statistics.

The M.L.S. program offered two broad areas of
specialization, the information science program and the
library science program, each encompassing a common core
but diverging widely in distribution requirements. The
information science track included such areas of

concentration as bibliometrics, information management, information retrieval and databases, and individualized instruction of which international studies was an option. Enrollment data for the fall semester of 1983 indicate that 25 students had chosen the information science specialty. The library science track, in which 30 students were enrolled in 1983, included archival administration, art librarianship, double-degree studies (in art, music, or history, for example), health sciences librarianship, law librarianship, music librarianship, public librarianship, and individualized studies by function, type of library, or international studies. The curriculum--excerpted from a proof of the bulletin that was never printed--was the product of an arduous, acrimonious revision process which led at least in part to the dismissal of one executive officer and is said by faculty and administrators alike to have been sufficient in itself as a cause of the school's demise.

"It was basically a problem of leadership," charged the associate vice president.

> The pathology began with the re-
> tirement of our late, great [executive
> officer.] After that we tended to
> make a couple of caretaking in-
> house appointments rather than
> looking outside. That's the wisdom
> of hindsight now.

One acting executive officer and two designated for that role, the "caretakers," according to the associate vice president, served the school between 1971 and 1980. In the latter year, a search for a new chief executive was successful in bringing to Delta an individual of great promise, chosen to ensure the school's continuing promi-nence in both instruction and research. One of his charges was to lead an immediate revision of the curriculum. As one faculty member took great pains to explain,

> We [already] had curriculum com-
> mittees who had been working on [a
> revision] for over a year. So it
> turned out that they felt that [the
> new executive officer] wanted to
> impose his ideas on them and they
> didn't think his ideas were so great.
> He, on the other hand, felt that
> things were moving too slowly and
> he was under a fair amount of pres-
> sure from the front office to get
> something done. Now unfortunately,
> I think too much was made of that
> curriculum. [The new executive
> officer] seemed to be telling the
> front office that we had a terrible
> curriculum and unless we had a
> better one we couldn't go and recruit
> or do this, that, or the other. I
> think that was a fallacy; of course
> we could recruit with what we had.
> [The curriculum] wasn't that bad. It
> was not very structured. We had
> gotten down to only two required
> courses, reference and cataloging.
> The faculty's feud with [the execu-
> tive officer] began with the cur-
> riculum. The other part of the
> problem was that he could not relate
> to people very well.

And, she added, "he made no effort to build up a constituency on the faculty." Another faculty member as-
serted that

> we never had a leadership to stand.
> An amorphous body, a faculty, can-
> not provide leadership as a body.

Yet the associate vice president disagrees:

> They [didn't] know how to act like a
> school. That was one of the prob-
> lems from the point of view of
> administrative dealings with them.
> It was democracy gone crazy over
> there--absolutely crazy! There was
> all this backbiting....They thought
> they owned the courses they taught
> and wouldn't permit them to be
> changed in any way.

Providing a different perspective is the faculty member
who admits to serious opposition to the executive officer's
management style.

> Eventually we drew up a bill of
> particulars and presented it to the
> president. Among others the par-
> ticulars were his total lack of direc-
> tion, total lack of accomplishment,
> his poor management and mis-
> management of ongoing work, and
> the deterioration of relations be-
> tween him and the faculty. All the
> faculty signed it except one who was
> about to retire. We recommended
> that [the executive officer] be
> relieved of his [administrative
> duties]...but not that he be relieved
> as professor.

Apparently as a result of that memorandum the
executive officer left his post, which he had occupied less
than two years. "It turns out there was a lawsuit," said a
faculty member.

> [The executive officer] had sued the
> university. There were a number of
> depositions. As a result there was a
> settlement which came out of the li-
> brary school's budget, which con-
> tributed to our considerable deficit.

Added another faculty member:

> He sued the university and he sued
> the president but he did not sue the
> library school. The suit was settled
> out of court and we got saddled with
> the court costs. And we were furi-
> ous about that in our budget that
> [was] already badly in deficit. We
> had to pay thousands of dollars.

Speaking in sharp disagreement to the foregoing is
the academic vice president, who still maintains that the
deposed executive officer was precisely the person who
could have turned the school around.

> When we hired him, we hired, rel-
> atively speaking, an unorthodox
> library school administrator. We
> hired a person whose management
> style was confrontational. We put
> that person inside a faculty of
> mostly tenured people who didn't
> want to be touched, talked to, or
> bothered in any way. And he began
> to swing his axe. [The faculty was]
> strong enough to convince first the
> president and then me that [the ex-
> ecutive officer] was the problem. A
> year after he had left I realized that
> he was obviously not the problem
> but more likely the solution.

Rather, the vice president speculated;

> The problem was the general in-
> transigence of the faculty. So we
> had this major upheaval....We had a
> leader talking about curricular
> reform and [a faculty] not wanting
> to talk about what they did within
> their own courses in sufficient detail
> to be sure of what they were going
> to try to reform. The faculty had
> just run amok.

The faculty's apparent unwillingness "to be touched, talked
to, or bothered in any way" was a symptom, according to
the vice president, of the library school's "extraordinary
insularity."

> There was hardly a single faculty
> member who was known to any
> other faculty member in any other
> professional school [of the univer-
> sity.] No one had met anyone from
> [the business school], the department
> of computer science, or the de-
> partment of management information
> systems....They didn't know where
> the computer labs were on campus.
> Insularity proved to be a disaster.

And, he added, "this is simply not the way to move ahead
in a field that calls itself interdisciplinary."

Meanwhile, as the curriculum revision was in a
state of flux and relations between the faculty and the then
executive officer continued to deteriorate, a team representing the Committee on Accreditation of the American
Library Association visited the campus for its periodic site
examination of the M.L.S. program in the spring of 1981.

The following June 30, it was voted by the membership of the Committee on Accreditation to accredit conditionally until July 1, 1983, the M.L.S. program. "We'd never had any trouble with being reaccredited before," remembered a faculty member; "we probably didn't take it seriously enough." It has been alleged that compiling information for the self-study document was delegated to a single faculty member, whose responsibility writing and producing the document it also became. Admitted another faculty member, "we shot ourselves in the foot." The report issued by the visiting team listed 22 recommendations. Excerpts appear below.

1. <u>Goals and Objectives</u>. Those should be clarified and specified for each element of the curriculum.

2. <u>Curriculum</u>. A major concern of the team. Revision should be completed as soon as possible. All faculty should review their areas of expertise 'to insure that the curriculum...provide for the study of the principles and procedures common to all types of libraries and library services and contribute to making the curriculum a unified whole.' Provision should be made for students and practitioners to participate in the review. Syllabi and course outlines should be updated.

3. <u>Faculty</u>. That vacancies be filled. That the school look at its faculty evaluation process as a tool for 'critical self-evaluation.' Faculty members should 'increase substantially' their participation in professional organizations.

4. <u>Students</u>. The school should ahere to admission and retention requirements that 'meet or exceed those of other graduate programs' of the university.

5. Governance. The school should strengthen
the [executive officer's] leadership to provide 'a
stronger focus for program development.'

6. Physical Resources and Facilities. Immediate steps should be taken to remedy deficiencies in the library school library and that it
be funded so that it meet the continuing needs
of the program. 'Unacceptable environmental
conditions' should be corrected. The school
should acquire on site dedicated terminals for
searching major bibliographic utilities
'appropriate to the learning needs of students in
its program.'

Said a faculty member;

It was the strangest action that COA
ever undertook; it was just a vicious
action. Unjustified. It's possible
that [the team] sensed we were in
the middle of an administrative
change and turmoil. It seems to me
that COA was subconsciously or
consciously itching to reassert itself.

More seriously he charged;

I can document very easily that there
were two points...that were totally
unjustified. [Things] were drummed
up. There were impressions; they
were not basic facts. For instance
one of the points was that the faculty doesn't have [its office] hours
posted on their doors. It turns out
that that was false.

Yet the executive officer did not appear at the orientation
meeting for students, faculty, and members of the visiting
team, and members of the team subsequently wrote that
they were "dismayed" by the poor attendance. "I think the
executive officer might have turned [the team] off," speculated a faculty member.

> I think both sides were at fault here.
> I think [the executive officer]
> thought he could use [the team] to
> whip the faculty into line; faculty
> thought they could use COA....The
> result was it backfired. It came as a
> terrible shock....

The academic vice president expressed a differing view;

> [Accreditation] is a necessary evil; I
> deal with accreditation teams all the
> time. If you really want it you play
> the game. We could have been ac-
> credited if the faculty had wanted it.
> The problem was they didn't take it
> seriously. The faculty didn't stay in
> their offices when they had ap-
> pointments with the team. I
> wouldn't accredit them either.

On June 30, 1982, the then executive officer's
service ended and a member of the faculty was appointed
to succeed him in an acting capacity the following day.
"We needed somebody who could go to the ALA and get
our accreditation back,"said the associate vice president,
"and she did the job for us beautifully."

The academic vice president:

> She was a good trooper; a fine
> leader. I liked her. Nobody is ap-

pointed to head a troubled program
as a reward. She sure didn't see it
as a plum. It was a matter of intel-
lectual respect that the university not
close down something as famous as
[the library school]. I [was not
going] to go to the Board and close
it because a professional school in
this university couldn't get accredited. I [was not going] to have
people say to me later, 'Well, the
reason you closed it was...you
couldn't get accredited.'

From all accounts, the final months of 1982
brought a concerted effort on the part of both vice presidents, the acting executive officer, and the faculty to have
the conditional accreditation removed, and thus full
accreditation restored, in advance of the July 1, 1983,
deadline. At the same time, steps were taken toward more
aggressive student recruitment, as it was believed that if
enrollment in the M.L.S. program--which would drop from
a recent FTE peak of 144 in 1976 to a low of 50 the following spring--could be increased, revenues would rise;
and perhaps the discussions about the future of the library
school which had begun to occur monthly at meetings of
the Trustees' executive committee, would cease.

In January of 1983 the acting executive officer, the
two academic vice presidents, and a member of the faculty
traveled to San Antonio to present the program's case for
reaccreditation to the Committee on Accreditation. Subject
to continued reporting on a brief list of items, the program
regained full accreditation six months before the deadline.
At that time the academic vice president also met with a
number of candidates for the full-time position of executive officer.

Trustees' concerns about the library school, however, were not alleviated by the vote of confidence that
had been expressed by COA. At issue, apparently, was the
school's continuing deficit spending; the shortfall was
estimated early in 1983 at some $290,000. The school's
financial difficulties were not new, though. In fact, a
1979 published history of Delta's library school mentions
"two decades of annual deficits" punctuated by budgetary
surpluses only four times during the 1970s. A bequest of
$2 million, earmarked as endowment funds by its donor, a
private foundation, was made to the library school in 1981.
First payments on the gift amounting to about $200,000,
viewed by many as a means of ensuring the school's future
financial security, had been received, with full payment to
be made by 1987. "And there was more money there," said
a faculty member.

> I was told by the president of [the
> foundation] that they were willing to
> go to various industrial and com-
> mercial enterprises in [the area] and
> ask for more money....If the univer-
> sity had only been willing to carry
> us for one more year....

The academic vice president dismisses the gift as the
godsend some thought it to be.

> That's nonsense: a sad comment on
> library education. It would have
> given us the largest endowment of
> any library school in America.
> We're talking about peanuts! Why,
> the income at what--six percent?
> That money could not have saved
> the school.

On February 1, 1983, the search for an executive
officer was terminated and the faculty member who had

been serving in an acting capacity assumed the permanent post. Faculty members are bitter about the academic vice president's continuing discussions with the Board, charging that the substance of those conversations was never communicated to them. "It seemed that there was all this stuff going on behind our backs," said one member of the faculty. By the time classes resumed the following autumn, however, discussion of the dual problems of dwindling enrollment and further loss of revenue had begun to dominate library school faculty meetings. The idea of a five-year plan was first proposed in mid-November, for earlier that month the associate vice president had requested from the faculty a planning statement to be used both for making decisions within the school and for seeking program support from the university and the community at large. Some of the topics the faculty was asked to consider included the nature of the student body; recruiting and financial aid; programmatic mix (the relationship between the library science and information science tracks); further development of faculty research interests; fund raising; and cost-cutting. The opportunity to fashion such a plan was evidently perceived by the faculty as a reprieve; and the associate vice president later wrote that the plan expressed "basically an optimistic and modestly expansionist" point of view.

"Reorganization," stated the document, "is a desirable and viable alternative to closing." It incorporated the following elements.

1. Refocusing and contraction of the M.S. in L.S. program with increased emphasis on information science.

2. A reduced faculty of six persons, each of whom would teach six courses per year.

3. Retention and restructuring of the doctoral program, making greater use of courses taught

in other departments. The library school would
offer five courses at the doctoral level.

4. Immediate offering of several undergraduate
courses in information science and the creation
of a bachelors program in that area.

5. Tailoring a continuing education program
more closely to local needs, especially on those
of industrial organizations.

A budget submitted with the plan called for expenditures
of $512,000, at least partially offset by income of $426,000
for the 1985-86 academic year. Consistent with its perception of "the changing information environment," the
faculty wrote that reorganization could serve as "a launch-
ing point for innovative and forward-looking programs on
a university-wide basis." From mid-December until mid-
January, the plan was circulated to a number of individuals in the university administration, and on January 11 the
academic vice president once again met with the executive
committee of the Board of Trustees.

Therefore it came as a surprise to the faculty that
when the vice president met with them on January 16, he
reported that the Trustees had made it clear that barring a
guarantee that the fiscal situation would improve immediately, "business as usual would not be the order of the
day." He then outlined four options for the school's future
that he would consider before making a final recommendation to the president at the end of January: to accept the
reorganization plan as submitted by the faculty; to continue
operations, scaled down with fewer faculty; to close the
school and relocate the faculty within the university; or to
create an interdisciplinary information science program on
both the graduate and undergraduate levels, dissolving the
M.S. in L.S. program. He later recalled that

the Chairman of the Board told me,
'we won't let you run [the library
school] forever; you have more to do
than to mind the store and see that
they don't buy too many
stamps.'...Yes, there was pressure
from above.

Immediately after the adjournment of the January
16 meeting, the vice president announced that all admissions to the school would be suspended indefinitely. Said
the associate vice president;

I was responsible for that. I mean,
pure and simple, it wasn't a gambit;
it wasn't a secret way to close the
school. It had nothing to do with
that. When we closed the education
department some years before, what
we discovered was that the big
problem we had was being taken to
court by students....Now, in theory if
our original scenario had played
itself out, it was a six-weeks'
suspension, or a two-months' suspension and then the issue was going
to be decided. But when we went to
the [faculty] senate we hit a buzzsaw.

A faculty member recalled that

some people believe that [the academic vice president] said it out in
the corridor after the meeting was
over. But no matter, the result was
the same. When it appeared in the
newspaper and in the library press
that [the library school] wasn't ac-

> cepting any more applications...well,
> once that appears in public print the
> school is finished. It was a *de facto*
> closing. It was an extraordinarily
> stupid thing to do. ...It was clear
> that from the day [the académic vice
> president] set foot in this place on
> January 16th that [closing the school]
> was his favorite option.

Inspired by the crisis, an emergency meeting of the
school's visiting committee, composed of alumni, local
practitioners, library educators and representatives from
industry, was called. The vice president noted that

> it was a stormy session; it lasted for
> two and a half hours. While [the
> committee] eventually recommended
> that the school be kept open for
> another year, they proposed some
> pretty radical things like asking [the
> executive officer] to resign, and
> asking that all the faculty renounce
> their tenure and take a 10 percent
> pay cut.

On February 14, the vice president once again visited the faculty, this time to inform them that he had recommended to the university administration that admissions
be suspended; that the school be closed on July 1, 1985;
that tenured faculty be given notices of termination effective June 30, 1986; and that a university-wide commission
be appointed to study the future of an interdisciplinary
information science program on the campus. He had made
such recommendations because, as he later reported, "I
[had] absolutely no faith that [any of the other options]
would have worked. The matter would then be turned
over to the faculty senate, perhaps by March; no group
would have veto power over his recommendation, however.

Thus the proceedings "hit the buzzsaw," as the associate vice president characterized the situation, for in March the faculty senate voted to reject the recommendation to close the school. What the senators proposed instead was that the problem be studied for another year. A newspaper article described other university faculty members as "miffed...that their role as advisers had been undercut." "I think it went deeper than that," said a member of the library school faculty;

> People in other schools and departments really feared that if the administration could do us in so easily, the same thing might happen to them. The faculty senators thought the administration had acted in a high-handed fashion and...had usurped the prerogatives of the senate...So the administration which had hoped to get a vote out of the Board of Trustees that spring was forced to postpone the issue.

Meanwhile the information science task force had begun its investigation. "We were excluded," said a faculty member;

> When the commission first met [the vice president] told them they were not to consider the matter of the library school; all they had to do was look at the role of information studies in society and decide the university should offer a program in information studies....They also got some money from the Council on Library Resources which I thought

>really was under false pretenses
>because they had no intention of
>discussing library science at all.

Explaining his viewpoint is the vice president.

>The library school didn't fall in love
>with [the task force] because they
>weren't the focal point of it. [The
>commission] was not charged with
>figuring out the future of the library
>school or the role of the library
>school but neither were they told to
>ignore the library school....Things
>they did look at were the idea of an
>undergraduate minor and where they
>could find a home for information
>studies at this university.

In the end, however, according to the vice president, "the whole thing fizzled out because it never got a champion." During the next 12 months, as the vice president's office continued to hold the library school in receivership, faculty members campaigned tirelessly to garner support from within the university, from thousands of alumni located around the world, and from the surrounding community. Those efforts were not to be successful.

In mid-January of 1985 the academic vice president distributed to the faculty senate a memorandum which he titled, "Summary of Rationale for Closure of [the library school.]" The field of library science, he wrote, is not growing; job opportunities exist only at replacement rates. Dwindling enrollments in library schools which have led in part to the closing of several programs still indicate an oversupply of library education programs. Moreover, the existence of a publicly-supported library school a short distance away has had a substantial affect on Delta's continuing decline in enrollment. Doubting that the future

holds sufficient promise (and remuneration) for attracting
to the profession high-quality students, he maintained that
the school's tuition (at approximately $8,200 per year) was
too high to make a library school viable at Delta. "To put
it bluntly," he wrote, "the field itself suffers from a
paucity of strong leaders." The exhaustive search for an
executive officer which had failed to produce an acceptable candidate was another danger signal, he said, noting
that the same situation obtained with respect to faculty, for
"a field in difficulty as library education admittedly is does
not always attract 'the best and the brightest' to the pro-
fessoriat." Even given unlimited resources, he concluded,
it would not be a good investment to keep the school open;
because

> there is virtually no evidence that
> we would find sufficient numbers of
> the kind of faculty we would want
> when present faculty retire, nor
> would we be likely to succeed in
> finding the kind of leadership that
> would be needed. And even if we
> could, there is no evidence that there
> are enough qualified students who
> would apply to and attend the school
> given the availability of much less
> expensive alternatives....It was
> ultimately for this reason--of which
> the school's financial situtation was
> and is merely symptomatic--that we
> should now act to close the [library
> school.]

Engaging in a thoughtful and spirited defense of the school
was a new executive officer, who had accepted the position at the resignation of her predecessor the previous
summer. She said of the vice president's "Rationale;"

> It was all a canard. There were no
> objective criteria. He dealt with
> non-issues. I think it was a rigged
> argument. My personal opinion now
> is that they wanted every single one
> of us gone. They decided years ago
> to get rid of us.

Following more vigorous debate in the faculty senate and a meeting of the entire university faculty, the
Board of Trustees voted on March 20, 1985, to close the
library school as of June 30, 1986. "It was like hearing that
your father had been killed," observed one faculty member.
Said the academic vice president;

> The reorganization came too late. It
> was totally unrealistic. You couldn't
> amortize the cost of our degree.
> Retrenchment? Absolutely not! If
> it were, there should have been
> other schools closed. When viewed
> on the micro level, the amount of
> money devoted to such a small pro-
> gram seemed large, but [financial]
> retrenchment never entered my
> mind. I never closed anything as an
> austerity move.

CHAPTER 3

ANALYSIS

As stated in Chapter 1, the objectives of the study were to identify conditions which were related to library school closings; and to determine the possible existence of a pattern of predisposing factors across the four programs that were examined by means of the case method. Through interviews with university officials, library school administrators, and library school faculty, and aided by documentary evidence both publicly available and heretofore undisclosed, the author sought to describe in narrative form the four library school closings as they were viewed by the parties involved.

The study's theoretical context posed six questions which were asked about each of the four library schools. Those included the following.

1. Was there evidence of an institutional financial crisis which called into question the future of academic programs including the Master of Library Science?

2. Were university administrators familiar with the mission and programs of the library school?

3. Did university administrators perceive a need for a library school on the campus?

4. Did the Master of Library Science program meet the 1972 *Standards* promulgated by the Committee on Accreditation of the American Library Association?

5. Did university administrators entertain alternatives other than closing the library school?

6. Was there an accredited M.L.S. program in the same
   state or region, or one nearby that extended in-
   state fee courtesy to out-of-state students?

   It became apparent during the course of the investigation that five more questions could be asked. Those
are listed below.

7. Were objective criteria, such as those suggested by the
   Vanderbilt Model and discussed in Chapter 1, employed in the decision-making process?

8. Had the library school recently engaged in curriculum
   reform?

9. Were the school's programs innovative?

10. Was there evidence of a turf battle, where faculty in
    other departments or schools perceived that library
    education programs had encroached upon their
    pedagogical territory?

11. Did university administrators view library school per-
    sonnel and programs as isolated from the rest of the
    academic community?

   As the four cases are compared and contrasted and
the above questions are answered based on the data gathered, it is important to reiterate two points that were
discussed in greater detail in Chapter 1. First, the case
study methodology precludes the establishment of direct
cause-and-effect linkages. Only one claim can be made:
certain conditions existed at the four universities prior to,
and at the time of, each program's elimination. Second,
the factors which obtained at the four universities studied
are not generalizable to any of the other universities where
M.L.S. programs have closed since 1978.

Question 1: <u>Evidence of a Financial Crisis</u>

Cuts in state funding were responsible for the shortfalls experienced by the two public universities, Beta and Gamma. In just a few years, Beta lost 30 percent of its state support; yet while the library school was closed, other programs--chiefly engineering, computer science, mathematics, and business--were strengthened and more generously allotted funding. "Reallocation," was the way one vice president characterized the university's response to its financial exigency. At Gamma a presidential recommendation to the governing board resulted in the paring of some $15 million from the $329 million operating budget in response to cuts in state funding that had begun during the 1970s. Such conditions prompted administrators to scrutinize programs and departments throughout the statewide system. "What can we pick off?" asked one of Gamma's administrators.

At Alpha, a private institution where operating funds are generated to a greater degree by the tuition paid by students than in public universities, the combination of declining enrollment and rising tuition contributed to a deficit projected to reach $6 million by the end of the 1984-85 academic year. As part of sweeping program reviews, during which officials decided to refocus the mission of the university on undergraduate education, the library school was closed. In contrast with the other three cases, Delta, a private university also faced with widespread enrollment declines and rising tuition, had not put into effect an overall retrenchment plan.

There is no doubt that each of the financial revalidation exercises was real; evidence confirming the existence of retrenchment on those campuses has been presented in this study and elsewhere. Yet funding does not tell the full story; despite such statements as "We were losing a bundle on [the library school]," (the president of

Alpha University), and a newspaper headline which stated that Delta's "library school's last chapter is the ledger."

More germane would appear to be reactions similar to that of Delta's academic vice president, who contended that the deficit which had been incurred by the library school on his campus was "symptomatic of [other] underlying pathologies." The four case narratives suggest that while financial exigency was the explicit reason for closing each program--and that which was given to the press and even library school personnel themselves--it was only the impetus that set in motion the decision-making process that was to culminate in the four schools' closings. In short, financial exigency was cited by university administrators to justify their actions when in reality their motives were much more complex.

"There was nothing...that was going to save [the library school]," remarked a Gamma University administrator. And the Delta vice president:

> Retrenchment never entered my
> mind. I never closed anything as an
> austerity move.

Moreover, library school personnel share the belief that was expressed by one of their ranks that

> if the administration had wanted to
> save the school, they would have.

Question 2: Administrators' Familiarity with Mission and Programs of the Library School

Due perhaps in part to their recent involvement in examination and evaluation of library education programs, all of the administrators interviewed demonstrated a high degree of familiarity with the schools' stated missions and goals. Some of those invididuals numbered librarians among members of their immediate families, and one had even worked for a time in a large public library. That is not to say that all of the persons involved in decision-making at all of the universities exhibited such familiarity, however. At Alpha, Gamma, and Delta, for example, faculty members from a variety of other departments and schools participated in the review process. Moreover, it cannot necessarily be assumed that administrators themselves were sufficiently familiar with the schools' missions and goals before the reviews began.

Alpha's executive officer expressed bitterness that the review panel charged with determining his school's future included no librarians. And when in the course of Alpha's program reviews the executive officer was given thirty minutes to present his case, he complained that he was not permitted adequate time to ensure a proper hearing. Had library school executives done an effective job of presenting their programs to their administrations before the reviews commenced?

Lines of disagreement are evenly drawn between administrators and executive officers. All of the executive officers interviewed maintained that if their upper managements had been truly familiar with, and respectful of, the aims of their schools, the programs would not have been eliminated. The frequent comment that "[they] would have saved the school if they had wanted to," warrants repeating.

Whose primary responsibility was it to see that administrators were kept apprised of the schools' aims and progress? The Gamma administrator to whom the executive officer of the library school reported recalled that he had so little contact with his subordinate as to "forget most of the time that the library school even existed." And even though Alpha's executive officer maintained that "I was over there [in the administration building] all the time," the administrator to whom he reported disputed the effectiveness of the executive officer's communication.

> What amazed me was that...most
> people beat a path to your door....He
> sort of retreated....

In a large university it is not unusual for a vice president's span of control, or the number of individuals reporting to that office, to exceed a dozen or more. At issue at the University of Beta was that the vice president's span of control was so great--and some have maintained that his interest in the library school was so slight--that the executive officer was in effect demoted to a reporting relationship with an associate vice president. As a result, that vice president recalled,

> I became very familiar with [what
> they were trying to do], and it
> wasn't working.

Delta's academic vice president, whose office held the library school in receivership for more than one year, reported that he became so familiar with the library school that he soon concluded,

> they weren't doing what they were
> supposed to be doing.

As a result, Beta and Delta administrators began to attempt to press their own views on the library schools. And as existing programs diverged more and more widely from what those administrators regarded as the great future potential for library education--a partial understanding acquired, for example, by Delta's vice president during his conversations with library educators, practitioners, and alumni as he searched at length for a new executive officer--the more uneasy coexistence became.

"They could have done so much with industry," said Gamma's administrator. "...They weren't interested in the way the world was changing." Delta's vice president agreed. Ultimately administrators at all four universities would share the view that the schools had not lived up to their potential. Such faulty communication proved to be disastrous. The third question is closely related.

Question 3: <u>Need for a Library School on the Campus</u>

Was there a need for a library school? All of the university administrators interviewed answered this question with an unequivocal "no," although in the circumstances they could scarcely be expected to answer the question in the affirmative. After Alpha's program review the library school was declared superfluous to the university's mission. Gamma's budget advisory panel asked which programs the university could do without, determining that the library school was one. At Beta the administration reallocated funds to other programs which had been assigned higher priority. Finally, Delta's vice president contended that publicly supported universities could do a better job of educating librarians than could private universities. Three factors figured prominently in those determinations: administrators' alarm over continuing declines in enrollment in library education programs, their perception of low demand for M.L.S. graduates, and their belief that library school personnel had failed to justify a need for their programs.

The fact that enrollment had declined in library schools all over the United States was seen by some decision-makers as evidence of lessened need for library education programs; although the vice presidents of the two private universities studied, Alpha and Delta, admitted that high tuition had driven away prospective students. "We priced ourselves out of the market," said one. "You couldn't amortize the cost of our degree," said another. Moreover, the administrators were aware of the proliferation of M.L.S. programs that had occurred during the 1960s and 70s. "It was not like getting rid of economics or English," said one Gamma administrator, implying that instruction in such subjects could not be done without. Indeed that sentiment was echoed by several informants: library education was dispensable.

Also contributing to those views was the widespread perception of a dearth of employment opportunities for professional librarians. Gamma's administrator was alone among others interviewed who still believed that his library school's graduates could find jobs, but even he expressed some surprise that they did:

> There wasn't any problem in place-
> ment [of graduates]; but there was a
> disjuncture between the curriculum
> and and placement....

It is almost as though he was saying that M.L.S. graduates found jobs in spite of the education that they had received.

One of the main points in Delta's rationale for closing its library school was, in the vice president's words,

> The field of library science is not
> growing; job opportunities exist only
> at replacement rates.

Dwindling enrollment, he observed, had led in part to the closing of several other library education programs in the United States, but it still indicated an oversupply of M.L.S. programs; that despite a vigorous effort by the executive officer of Delta's library school to mount a reasoned and informative denial of that point of view.

Most serious of all, however, was that several of
the administrators who were interviewed maintained that
library school executives and faculty had been unable to
convince management that their programs were necessary.
Those same persons were regarded by one administrator as

> out of date. But there was some-
> thing more here that was more than
> tiredness; there was dead wood in
> the sense of not being interested in
> the way the world was chang-
> ing....We couldn't restructure the
> program; we had to kill it.

Gamma's administrator:

> We wrote a report saying that the
> library school is not up to quality.
> [The then executive officer] and a
> few people came over and wanted
> me to explain that. After I ex-
> plained it, they left. They didn't
> oppose it.

Question 4: Compliance with 1972 Accreditation Standards

Were the programs "up to quality?" The evidence
suggests that qualitative standards used in the internal
evaluations of the four library schools were different and
perhaps more stringent than those promulgated and applied
by the Committee on Accreditation of the American
Library Association.

Quality was not an issue in the closing of Alpha's
library school. That university's program review panel had
considered the quality of the library school, apparently

giving it high marks. Not only had Alpha's M.L.S. program been fully reaccredited in 1980, it also had enjoyed high ratings in a recent perception study.

Gamma's program had been fully reaccredited in 1981 as well, but in its case doubts concerning the school's quality, based on two non-COA reviews which predated the final reaccreditation by six years, apparently lingered on in the minds of decision-makers. Both of those reports described faculty research productivity as "weak," presumably in comparison with some perception of a national research standard. The Committee on Accreditation, however, found much that was praiseworthy about Gamma's program, including its "carefully constructed" and "unified" curriculum and "good" faculty research productivity.

Delta's problems with the Committee on Accreditation were detailed in Chapter 2. Critically important to an understanding of that program's plight are the academic vice president's words.

> I [was not going] to go to the Board
> and close [the library school] because
> a professional school in this univer-
> sity could not get accredited. I [was
> not going] to have people say to me
> later, 'Well, the reason you closed it
> was...you couldn't get accredited.'

A cooperative effort joined by library school personnel and university administrators regained full accreditation for the M.L.S. program at Delta, yet the school was closed two years later.

Only at the University of Beta was accreditation an issue in the program's demise. When library school personnel were advised not to appeal COA's 1983 decision not to reaccredit the masters program, and the administration declined to invest the sum of $150,000 in a reaccreditation effort two years hence, the school was closed. A vice president wrote that the expenditure did not seem "wise," in view of the fact that

> there is no certainty that we would [re]gain accreditation.

He called the possibility of offering an unaccredited program "unrealistic," for decline would almost surely accelerate. "[Accreditation] is the key, your mark of outside sanction," he maintained. When Beta's review panel had announced its program priority decisions several months previously, only a vigorous appeal by library school personnel saved the program from immediate phase-out. Its priority 3, or "decrease resources and/or merge..." rating, followed so closely by the decision not to contest the COA ruling, however, sealed the school's fate only a short time later.

Question 5: Alternate Options

The decision to close Alpha's library school came at the culmination of program review and as the university's mission was refocused to emphasize undergraduate education. Other units that were eliminated included the theater department, the school of nursing, undergraduate programs in speech pathology and education, and the department of anthropology. All were declared irrelevant to the university's new mission. It is important to note that mission redefinition frequently accompanies retrenchment; presidents and boards of trustees are vested with the power to alter an institution's mission as are officers and faculty of library schools and other academic units to redefine theirs.

At the University of Beta four options were entertained by academic officers before closing the library school. The first was to mount an appeal to the Committee

on Accreditation, even though an outside consultant had
determined that such an effort would be ill-advised; in his
report to the library school he termed COA's decision
"incontestable." Second was to seek reaccreditation in two
years. Third was to continue operating an unaccredited
program indefinitely. That however, wrote the vice president, would ensure continuing decline and further drains
on resources. The fourth was to close the school, despite
the vice president's view that the library school

> [had] served so well in a valuable
> role and whose graduated [had] con-
> tributed in many ways and places to
> their profession.

Administrators at Gamma University simply closed
the library school and a number of other programs
throughout the statewide system. Some months after the
announcement that library education would be eliminated,
however, a university task force was formed to investigate
the future of information studies on the campus. One
member of the task force remembered that for a time, the
panel debated retaining at least a vestige of the library
school's mission in a new center for information studies.
Eventually, though, the idea failed to win the necessary
support, and in the words of an administrator, the efforts
of the task force were "an abortion."

Late in 1983, the faculty of Delta's library school
presented to administrators and trustees a document which
outlined a plan for reorganizing the program. The plan
featured a refocusing of the masters degree on information
science; a reduced faculty; restructuring of the Ph.D. program; undergraduate course offerings; and a redoubled
effort at continuing education. The following January the
vice president visited a library school faculty meeting and
outlined four options he would consider before making a
final recommendation to the president. Those included the
following: to accept the faculty's reorganization plan; to

continue operating with fewer faculty; to close the library
school and relocate faculty elsewhere in the university; and
to create an interdisciplinary information science program.
In an action similar to that taken at Gamma, the library
school was closed and an information science task force
was empaneled. It, too, failed to devise a solution because,
as the vice president remembered,

> The whole thing fizzled out because
> it never got a champion.

Many library school personnel expressed bitterness
over the way the decisions were made, apparently believing
that the program reviews that were conducted and the
alternatives presented were window-dressing to justify
immutable decisions that had already been made. Said one
faculty member,

> It was as though they'd already de-
> cided to kill the library school and
> made up the standards to be sure
> we'd be unable to meet them.

And the executive officer of Alpha's library school bluntly
stated;

> I think they could have done the
> whole thing without throwing in the
> [program] evaluations. I think the
> program evaluations, frankly, were
> eyewash to back-stop preconceived
> notions of what it is they intended
> to do in the first place.

Question 6: Nearby M.L.S. Programs

In three of the four cases--Beta, Gamma, and
Delta--the presence of M.L.S. programs at public institutions in neighboring states was cited by decision-makers
to justify closing their library schools. Administrators
maintained that since other programs were available a
comparatively short distance away, their institutions need
not operate library schools. The notion that the number of
library education programs in the United States exceeds
student demand figured prominently in those decisions.

Within Beta's state was another larger and more
prestigious program, and extension courses offered by a
large school in a contiguous state were available within
several hours' drive. One of Gamma's administrators noted
that

> while the library school has the only
> accredited program in the state, two
> unaccredited programs exist [in the
> state] and neighboring states to the
> east and south also have accredited
> programs.

Steps to arrange in-state fee structures for students from
Gamma's state were apparently taken by one official of
one of those accredited programs. Only 20 miles from
Delta's campus was a growing M.L.S. program at a publicly
supported institution, and it was to that university that
adminstrators looked to "pick up the slack." Alpha's program stood alone, however, not only in its state but also in
a geographic region where the number of library schools is
small.

While it cannot be said that the loss of Beta,
Gamma, and Delta's library education programs will not be
felt by alumni, practitioners, and prospective students in
three very populous areas, other M.L.S. programs do exist

nearby. That such a rationale was employed, however, is unlikely to mollify prospective students and others who looked to those library schools for professional guidance and support. The library community in Alpha's region will be hardest hit.

Question 7: Objective Criteria

The Vanderbilt Model described in Chapter 1 provided a framework useful for evaluating the program reviews that were conducted at three of the institutions studied--Alpha, Beta, and Gamma. Criteria developed by officials of Alpha and Gamma Universities were clearly articulated and although not so extensive as those formulated at Vanderbilt University, bear more than passing similarity to Vanderbilt's. Both also involved redefinition of the universities' missions. The reader is referred to the case study reports for greater detail.

At issue is whether or not the evaluation criteria were employed in a straightforward manner. Some of the library school personnel who were interviewed believed that they were not; for as one faculty member contended,

> ...They made up the standards to be
> sure we'd be unable to meet them.

Not surprisingly, administrators at Alpha and Gamma vehemently denied that and similar charges.

Beta's financial losses prompted university officials to reallocate funding from programs like the library school to others which were given higher priority in an institution-wide evaluation. Numerical priorities eventually arrived at would determine whether a program would be strengthened, maintained at the present level, resources decreased or merged, or phased out. The library school first received word that it would be phased out; only after considerable effort on the part of its executive and faculty was its priority raised one increment. While it is indisputable that an evaluation was conducted, no one interviewed at the University of Beta was able to produce documentation that specified what, if any, the evaluation criteria were.

At Delta University neither were criteria developed nor did a program evaluation occur. Remembered the vice president,

> I didn't think we needed any. We'd
> just had two reviews by ALA that
> pretty much told the story.

When asked why he did not fashion some objective standards for no other reason than to justify his recommendation to the president, he replied that in the circumstances such standards were unnecessary.

Question 8: <u>Curriculum Reform</u>
Question 9: <u>Curriculum Innovation</u>

The two questions are combined for the purposes of analysis. Both ask what role library school curricula might have played in decisions to eliminate the programs.

The situations that obtained at Beta and Gamma are similar: by all accounts the curriculum review process at the two schools was both conservative and gradual. As a result, perhaps, decision-makers regarded both programs as out of date. Gamma's administrator called the library school "out of step with the times," although he admitted that the recent addition of two faculty members had been beneficial to its curriculum. And whereas Beta's program had in earlier years enjoyed some prominence in school

library and media studies, its course offerings, too, were
viewed by university officials as "tired."

The information science program at the University
of Delta had once been among the most highly regarded of
its type, but as Delta's curriculum was emulated by other
schools where equipment, for example, was more generously funded, it was badly in need of revision by the late
1970s. When a new executive officer was hired, his first
duty was to preside over a complete revamping of the curriculum. As described in Chapter 2, many observers
believe that the ensuing dispute which arose between the
executive officer and the faculty occurred largely over the
complex and acrimonious issue that curriculum reform
became. And that battle, in turn, is regarded by library
school personnel as a major cause of the school's demise.

The ambitious new information management concept proposed by the executive officer of Alpha's library
school was one of a handful of similar programs in the
United States. Eschewing some of the more traditional
library education philosophies, the executive officer boldly
outlined a College of Information Management designed to
appeal to a "new breed" of information professional. That
the concept was innovative and even futuristic, in library
education terms, cannot be denied, yet the program failed
to win university support. One administrator who was
interviewed ruefully spoke of the executive officer's
"throwing the baby out with the bath water;" apparently
expressing his personal regret that the needs of students
who sought careers in more traditional areas of librarianship might not be served by the new program. Moreover,
university officials agreed that the executive officer had
presented his plans for a drastic overhaul of the library
school at a time when the university could least afford
such expansion, despite the executive officer's financial
projections demonstrating how the information management idea could become self-supporting and eventually
contribute additional funds to the university's coffers.

Question 10: Turf Battle

A problem facing any program that is as interdisciplinary as library and information science is the extent to which it can expand into new areas without being perceived as threatening to faculty into whose instructional territory the program is seen to intrude. The perception of library schools' intrusion into such established areas as computer science, systems analysis, and management information systems occurred at three of the universities that were studied.

Alpha faculty members in the departments of mathematics and computer science as well as the school of business apparently took umbrage at the library school's intent to become the College of Information Management. One of Alpha's administrators observed that the library school was "stepping on toes," although the executive officer has maintained that he "sat down repeatedly" with outside faculty in an attempt to establish cooperative relationships. The executive officer charged that he lost his turf battle because

> one of the problems you have...is not wanting to send your students somewhere else. [If] you have 500 credits to generate...you don't want to send 300 of them to some other department.

"[The library school] certainly did not have the status," remarked the vice president, "...as being qualified to teach what we call information management." None of the parties involved, however, was able to agree on what information management is or should be at Alpha University or elsewhere.

A turf battle also occurred at Beta. There conflict arose between the library school and the school of business, after business school faculty apparently determined that library education courses encroached upon their instruction in management information systems. Several of Beta's library school personnel commented that the business faculty members' fears were ill-founded; at the same time, however, expressing regret that none of their numbers had been able to convince either the business faculty or certain university administrators that such fears actually were groundless.

Turf battles at Gamma and Delta began only after the announcements of the two library schools' imminent demise and after the information studies task forces were formed. Some of Delta's library school personnel have maintained that they were betrayed by the task force. The vice president contended instead that

> the library school didn't fall in love
> with [the task force] because they
> weren't the focal point of it. [The
> task force] was not charged with
> figuring out the future of the library
> school but neither were they told to
> ignore [the library school.]

At Gamma as well, members of the task force were unable to reach an accommodation; and once again, it seemed, no one could be certain of either what information studies are, or whose instructional responsibility they should be.

Question 11: Isolation of the Library School

All four library schools--and their personnel--were viewed as isolated, and insulated, from their local academic communities. Alpha's vice president remembered his association with the executive officer of his library school:

> Most people beat a path to your
> door....He sort of retreated...; he
> didn't build any bridges.

One of Gamma's administrators said that on his campus

> the library school had become iso-
> lated...and was not participating.
> People didn't know them in a social
> way. They knew them in a scholarly
> way, but as being out of date.

Beta's vice president agreed. And finally, Delta's vice
president concluded that

> [the library school's] insularity
> proved to be disastrous....This is
> simply not the way to move ahead in
> a field that calls itself interdisci-
> plinary.

A summary of the foregoing analysis is presented
in tabular form on the following page.

QUESTION

	ALPHA	BETA	GAMMA	DELTA
1. Financial crisis	Yes	Yes	Yes	Yes
2. Familiarity with mission and goals	Yes	Yes	Yes	Yes
3. Need	No	No	No	No
4. Compliance with Standards	Yes	No	Yes	No/Yes
5. Alternate options	No	Yes	No	Yes
6. Nearby programs	No	Yes	Yes	Yes
7. Objective criteria in evaluation	Yes	Yes	Yes	No
8. Curriculum reform	Yes	No	No	Yes
9. Innovativeness	Yes	No	No	No
10. Turf battle	Yes	Yes	Yes	Yes
11. Isolation	Yes	Yes	Yes	Yes

CHAPTER 4

SUMMARY AND CONCLUSIONS

It was the aim of the present study to describe in detail the circumstances which culminated in the closing of four library education programs between 1982 and 1985. Case study reports, which provided the first complete written accounts of those closings, constituted Chapter 2. Emphasis was placed on the perceptions of the parties involved as they recalled the events that transpired on their campuses. University administrators were key informants, as it was they who ultimately recommended to their trustees that the programs be targeted for elimination. The theoretical context of the study, presented in Chapter 1, generated questions and provided a framework for analysis, and the four cases were compared and contrasted in Chapter 3.

It has been demonstrated that the four closings were institution-specific; that is, each resulted from a series of events that was unique to each university. Yet, as the discussion in Chapter 3 attests, common factors were identified. A number of conclusions can be drawn.

Conclusions

It is an oversimplification to conclude that the four library schools were closed solely for financial reasons; although initially perhaps, that is what university officials would have desired interested parties, including the press, to believe. The late 1970s brought some form of financial retrenchment, whether or not so labeled by administrators, to the vast majority of university campuses in the United States. Some of the factors which precipitated retrenchment were discussed in Chapter 1. The four universities studied were not exempt from the particular pressures which declining enrollment, changing student populations, rising tuition, and dwindling resources exerted on them. Moreover, ample evidence suggests that in each of the four cases, financial reversals--on the university level, the library school level, or both--and institutional responses to those straitened conditions, first prompted the scrutiny and evaluation of library education programs. None of the university administrators who agreed to be interviewed, however, and few of the library educators, stated that the schools were closed as part of institutional belt-tightening. The closings were not retrenchment decisions, but political decisions.

The four case studies demonstrate a fundamental lack of understanding and communication between and among the library educators and their university managers; and in each of the four cases, to one extent or another, such difficulties were long-standing and relations bitter. Library educators at the four schools held the belief that their administrations had been "out to get them" for some years before the termination decisions were finally made. Both Chapters 2 and 3 elaborate on that point. It is as though university administrators merely tolerated their library schools ("We weren't doing anybody any harm," allowed one faculty member), neither giving them undue attention nor ignoring them entirely, until fiscal constraints gave rise to program evaluation, which in turn provided administrators and trustees with justification to close the schools. And restructuring the programs was not an option entertained very seriously, for as one administrator re-marked, "We couldn't restructure it; we had to kill it;" apparently reflecting his sentiments that his university had supported a weak program long enough. "Weak sister," in fact, was a term used by one administrator to describe the library school on his campus which he and others had countenanced in earlier, and better, times.

Some library educators concerned about the spate of library school closings have suggested that library schools are easy targets for elimination because of their largely female, low-status constitutencies. Parallels have been drawn with nursing and social work as other examples of female-dominated fields whose education programs have also been under siege on many campuses. Such a contention was supported by the data gathered in that the library schools' constituencies were scarcely considered at all, whereas alumni and practitioners might have been had the future of law, medical, or business schools been in question. Yet it seems that the invisible-constituency idea did not figure so prominently in the administrators' decision-making processes as did their perceptions of deep-seated problems ("pathologies," in the words of one administrator) within the schools themselves; problems that the administrators were unwilling to try to ameliorate--financially or programatically or by hiring new faculty to rebuild the schools from within.

In none of the four cases did university managers see a need for a library school on their campuses. The notion that the number of library schools in the United States greatly outstrips student demand was shared by administrators at all four universities. Other nearby programs could take up the slack--and meet what there was of student demand--when their schools closed, administrators at three of the universities maintained in their rationales for closing. Many still believed that jobs for librarians are in short supply. When some of the library educators labored to correct those misconceptions, their low credibility prevented them from swaying administrative opinion in any way, regardless of the cogency and vitality of some of their arguments.

Similarly, library educators were unable to convince their managers that the M.L.S. programs should be retained and strengthened. They themselves could not demonstrate why library education is necessary. If library educators could not testify to a need for their programs, then who could? It would appear that at least in part, the library educators' inability to justify their programs stems from a profession-wide uncertainty as to what it is that library schools should teach; despite recent efforts either from the library educators' standpoint, to propose a more standardized curriculum for the M.L.S., or from the practitioners', to identify basic professional "competencies."

Where turf battles entered into the decisions to close, the library schools were seen as encroaching on the pedagogical territory of other schools and departments. In particular, business, computer science, and management information systems faculty became alarmed that library school curricula threatened their own course offerings. More germane, perhaps, than the fact that the library education programs did in actuality not threaten other departments to any serious extent was that library school personnel were evidently unable either to define their instructional domain or to explain to the satisfaction of influential outsiders what the business of education for the information professions is all about.

Quality, as determined by the 1972 *Standards* promulgated and administered by the Committee on Accreditation of the American Library Association, was an issue in only one of the four closings, the University of Beta's. Yet the *Standards* remain the accepted benchmark by which the library profession judges its own education programs. In one case, that of Gamma University, two non-COA evaluations which in one administrator's words "told [the library school] to shape up or ship out" were followed some years later by full ALA reaccreditation. And in its report the site-visit team praised some of the features of the program which the earlier evaluators had found wanting.

Although it is irrelevant for this investigator to try to judge which standards were "better" or more ap-

propriate, it is not difficult to determine that the non-
COA evaluations were more critical. Moreover, in
Gamma's case, it was the non-COA evaluations that were
remembered by university administrators, while the library
educators chose to cite the more recent COA reaccreditation as an indicator of the quality of the program. The
evidence overwhelmingly indicates that in all four of the
cases, accreditation by the American Library Association
did not, and could not, guarantee the survival of library
education programs on campuses where administrators had
determined to eliminate them.

A serious charge leveled against the four defunct
programs is that their executives and faculty were isolated
from their academic peers. Neither socially nor academi-
cally were library educators known to any degree by their
colleagues, it was said. Where library educators had served
on university committees, some were perceived as being
out of date. In at least four instances, it would appear,
library educators maintained stronger ties with the professional practice than with their own universities and faculty
colleagues. Whether or not the educators' relative dissocia-
tion from their academic communities was related in some
way to the closings cannot be known. Perhaps some of the
educators failed to build bridges from some reluctance (or
inability) to "explain library and information science," as
several of the faculty informants complained was necessary
when they met with "outsiders." Library educators can no
longer afford to be isolated from their universities. What
occurred at Alpha, Beta, Gamma, and Delta demonstrates
why that is so.

The relation between the four schools' curricula
and the subsequent closings is unclear. It cannot be concluded that an innovative curriculum, for example, jeopard-
izes a library education program to a greater extent than
does a traditional one. A more salient factor was how the

curriculum was viewed by university administrators: three were regarded as outmoded and one, Alpha's, as too radical a departure from the past.

It is extremely disturbing that library education programs were so easily eliminated as university officials reshaped the missions of their institutions. The new mission at his university, said one faculty informant, "simply defined us out of business." Many of the library educators interviewed expressed dismay at what they regarded as the arbitrary nature of the mission-redefinition process. More than one suggested that when formal program evaluations took place, the criteria established by administrators were fabricated to ensure that the library school could not meet them. While it cannot be determined whether or not those suspicions are correct--as university administrators and library school personnel were evenly divided on either side of the issue--it would appear that mission-redefinition was employed by administrators as an additional justification for eliminating programs they no longer chose to operate.

Differentiating between circumstances which may have been related to the closings of public library schools and private ones was not an objective of the study. Indeed, the evidence presented in Chapter 3 has shown that in the balance, Alpha and Delta, the privately supported library schools, were strikingly similar to their public counterparts, Beta and Gamma.

Library schools in the United States are in grave danger of elimination by university administrators whose prerogative it is to redefine their institutions' missions to the exclusion of education for library and information science. Administrators interviewed in the course of the present study saw no need for library education programs as they currently exist, although some informants acknowledged, at least, the great potential which the field still possesses as society becomes increasingly dependent upon information and by implication, the services per-

formed by information intermediaries. Administrators had
given up on their library schools, however, as was demonstrated both by their reluctance to make investments of
time or resources necessary to restructure them, and by the
failure of information studies task forces to arrive at
workable strategies for change. Faced with pressure to
"cut something," administrators chose to eliminate their
library schools.

Observations

It has been noted that accreditation by the American Library Association cannot guarantee the survival of a
library education program on a campus where administrators have determined to eliminate it. Moreover, the internal evaluations to which library schools were subject were
apparently more critical than the 1972 *Standards* for
Accreditation. Two questions must be asked. First, are
the *Standards* adequate determinations of quality in situations where administrators are increasingly critical of
library education programs? And second, is the process
itself sufficiently reliable and valid so as to ensure that
each program has an equitable review by the Committee on
Accreditation?

To the extent to which university administrators
judge programs in terms of funds raised, grant-seeking by
library educators falls short of that engaged in by academics in other fields perhaps because of the widespread
notion that funding for research in library and information
science is unavailable. In comparison with funding that
many library schools received during the 1960s and 1970s,
times are indeed hard. Some of the educators interviewed
had assured their administrators that since funding is so
scarce, they had not attempted to seek it. Yet library
educators--several, notably, at Gamma University and the
University of Delta--were successful in obtaining grants

from private and public sources through creative, imaginative grantsmanship. While it is unlikely that all library schools will ever be self-supporting (and in fact such expectations expressed by university administrators are unrealistic in some circumstances), educators must continue to seek new funding sources.

Grant-seeking before university funding bodies that allocate resources intra-institutionally must increase as well. Library research has been largely ignored or overlooked due perhaps to educators' inability to demonstrate a need for their research or, more problematically, the salience of that work. And it might be argued that some of what has passed as library research is less than salient. Similarly, some library schools suffer from low prestige and low priority in the institutional budgeting process because their spokespersons have been unable to speak aggressively for their own interests. The competitive fiscal environment in which library schools reside calls for regular and vigorous self-justification by library educators.

Some educators have failed to articulate a need for their programs either because they are unable to do so or because perhaps they themselves are not certain of that need. Library schools lost turf battles when educators could not effectively explain, for example, how and why their course offerings did not overlap with business or computer science curricula. The service component in librarianship is one that may have been lost sight of in some library schools' haste to be up-to-date technologically. Yet service, the cornerstone on which librarianship was founded, is one aspect of the profession that is unique, which sets it apart from data processing and computer science; and one that must be pointed to with pride and renewed emphasis if library schools are to survive.

The library school leader will increasingly be called upon to be a diplomat, an ambassador to the university hierarchy, engaged in the regular activity of self-

justification of his or her program. Administrators themselves will continue to need to be shown why education for
the information professions is significant for society and
likely to become more so in the future. It is evident from
the events that occurred at Alpha University, the University of Beta, Gamma University, and the University of
Delta, that library educators failed at that most critical
task.

Library education programs that survive will share
two attributes: imaginative, diplomatic leadership and a
strong mission, or "sense of self." The case studies demonstrated the extent to which the four defunct programs fell
short in both of those areas. How can a library school gain
a sense of self? Published mission statements are clearly
not enough; all four of the programs had mission statements which had been revised shortly before the closings
were ordained. In part, library educators at the four
schools were unable to prove a need for their programs
because they, as do other educators at library schools that
have thus far escaped termination, remain uncertain about
what library schools should teach and why education for
the information professions should be a priority item on
campuses where library schools continue to exist.

Library educators frequently debate the question of
whether or not their field is a discipline. The number of
answers to that question is equalled only by the number of
participants in the debate. Persuasive arguments have been
voiced by all sides. As library education faces the most
serious crisis--and the most exciting opportunity--in its
hundred-year history, however, debating what library and
information science is called has acquired considerably less
importance than deciding what library and information
science is. For if library educators cannot explain what it
is they teach and why, someone else--typically university
administrators--will tell them. And it may be that they
will be told to teach nothing at all.

Opportunities for Further Research

A limitation of the present study is that it has investigated the closings of only four library schools. Eight other schools have closed since 1978, and it is possible that more programs will be eliminated in the future. Therefore a study which described other library school closings would be a useful addition to the literature; particularly if the findings of the present study were incorporated in the theoretical framework and used to generate questions or hypotheses.

Library schools are not alone among professional education programs that are in jeopardy. Schools of nursing, social work, pharmacy, and departments of speech pathology, for example, have also been widely eliminated. A study of the closings of other professional degree programs, perhaps comparing the data subsequently gathered to the findings of this study, might illuminate to a greater extent some of the factors associated with the termination of professional degree programs in general.

Equally useful would be a study comparing surviving library schools with those that have closed. How do the programs differ? How can library educators respond to and protect themselves from peremptory program reviews? What are some of the characteristics manifested by programs that survive? In short, what are the attributes and components of a successful library school?

Is the accreditation process sufficiently reliable and valid to ensure that each program has an equitable review? Does the process measure what it purports to? Do the membership of the Committee on Accreditation and library educators at large know what the *Standards* purport to measure?

While it was noted in Chapter 1 that the general literature on academic program evaluation was not chosen as a theoretical context for this study, an opportunity exists to compare one or more of the models with the evaluations that were made of the defunct schools. Moreover, the *Standards* for Accreditation could be compared with those models.

Another type of model, The Academic Institution-Building Model, developed at Indiana University, has been used there to investigate the closings of small liberal arts colleges. That model, notable because of its potential for quantifying institutional data along a number of ratings scales, could be tested on surviving library schools as a part of the planning process to determine future directions for those programs. Other institutional life-cycle models like Levine's might also be used to study both defunct programs and ones that have survived.

Finally, the question of what library and information science is cannot be answered in a study such as this one. Yet what it is that library schools teach, and why, remains the most compelling issue the study has raised. It is a matter of gravest consequence to the future of both library education and perhaps even the profession itself, that educators, practitioners, and other interested parties work together to formulate answers. The time to begin is now.

BIBLIOGRAPHY

American Association of Library Schools. *Library Education Statistical Report 1980*. State College: American Association of Library Schools, 1980.

Association for Library and Information Science Education. *Library and Information Science Education Statistical Report 1984*. State College: Association for Library and Information Science Education, 1984.

Backstrom, Charles H. and Hursh-Cesar, Gerald. *Survey Research*, 2nd ed. New York: John Wiley & Sons, 1981.

Beeman, Alice L. "Wilson College: A Case Study." Paper delivered at a Lilly Endowment Seminar for Indiana Independent Colleges and Universities, Indianapolis, 1979.

Blau, Peter M. *The Organization of Academic Work*. New York: John Wiley & Sons, 1973.

Bidlack, Russell E. Report to the Dean of the Graduate School of Indiana Unversity. Mimeographed, 1985.

Bogdan, Robert C. and Biklen, Sari Knopp. *Qualitative Research for Education: An Introduction to Theory and Methods*. Boston: Allyn and Bacon, 1982.

Borton, W.W. and Whalen, J.J. Untitled Manuscript, 1981.

Carmines, Edward G. and Zeller, Richard A. *Reliability and Validity Assessment*. Beverly Hills: Sage Publications, 1979.

Chamberlain, Philip C. "An Assessment of the Administrative and Decision Making Structures of Fontbonne College." Mimeographed, 1983.

Clark, David L. "In Consideration of Goal-Free Planning: The Failure of Traditional Planning Systems in Education." *Educational Administration Quarterly* 17(3):42-60 (Summer 1981).

Debons, Anthony and King, Donald W. *The Information Professional: Survey of an Emerging Field.* New York: Marcel Dekker, 1981.

Deutsch, Jerome M. "Retrenchment: Crisis or Challenge." *Educational Record* 64(1):41-44 (Winter 1983).

Doyle, K.J. "Managing Higher Education in a Climate of Contraction: A Conceptual Model." *Journal of Tertiary Educational Administration* 2(2):139-149 (October 1980).

Dyer, Esther and O'Connor, Daniel. "Crisis in Library Education." *Wilson Library Bulletin* 57(6):860-863 (June 1983).

Eshelman, William R. "Death at an Early Age: Library Schools in Oregon and California in Jeopardy." *Wilson Library Bulletin* 51(10):794 (June 1977).

Eshelman, William R. "The Erosion of Library Education." *Library Journal* 108(6):1309-1312 (July 1983).

Frances, Carol. "The Financial Resilience of American Colleges and Universities." *New Directions for Higher Education* no. 38 (Successful Responses to Financial Difficulty.) 10(2):113-120 (June 1982).

Glaser, Barney and Strauss, Anselm L. *The Discovery of Grounded Theory: Strategies for Qualitative Research.* New York: Aldine Publishing Co., 1967.

Goldhor, Herbert. *An Introduction to Scientific Research in Librarianship.* Urbana: University of Illinois Graduate School of Library Science, 1972.

Griffiths, José -Marie. "Microcomputers and Online Activities." *ASIS Bulletin* 10(4):13-14 (April 1984).

Hammond, Martine F. "Organizational Response for Survival: A Case Study in Higher Education." Paper delivered at the Annual Meeting of the Association for the Study of Higher Education, Washington, D.C., 1981.

Hardy, Cynthia. "The Management of University Cutbacks: Politics, Planning, and Participation." *Canadian Journal of Higher Education.* 14(1):59-69 (Winter 1984).

Healy, R.M. and Peterson, V.T. "Trustees and College Failure: A Study of the Role of the Board in Four Small College Terminations." Mimeographed, 1976.

Hyatt, James A. et al . *Reallocation; Strategies for Effective Resource Management.* Washington, D.C.: National Association of College and University Business Officers, 1984.

Kidder, Louise H. *Research Methods in Social Relations*, 4th ed. New York: Holt, Rinehart & Winston, 1981.

Learmont, Carol L. and Van Houten, Stephen. "Placements and Salaries 1983: Catching Up." *Library Journal* 109(17):1805-1811 (October 15, 1983).

Levine, Charles H. "More on Cutback Management: Hard Questions for Hard Times." *Public Administration Review* 39(2):179-183 (March/April 1979).

Levine, Charles H. "Organizational Decline and Cutback Management." *Public Administration Review* 38(4): (July/August 1978).

Matarazzo, James M. "Closing the Corporate Library: Case Studies on the Decision-Making Process." (Ph.D. Dissertation, University of Pittsburgh, 1979).

McClure, Charles R. "The Planning Process: Strategies for Change." *College and Research Libraries* 39: 456-466 (November 1978).

McIntyre, K.J.H. "Preparing for College Closing." *Educational Record*. 290-298 (Summer 1977).

Miles, Matthew B. and Huberman, A. Michael. *Qualitative Data Analysis: A Sourcebook of New Methods.* Beverly Hills: Sage Publications, 1984.

Miller, James L. and Erwin, J. Michael. "Analysis of College Closings." Paper delivered at the Annual Meeting of the Association for the Study of Higher Education, Washington, D.C., 1982.

Millett, J.D. *Mergers in Higher Education: An Analysis of Ten Case Studies.* Washington, D.C.: American Council on Education, 1976.

Mingle, James R. and Associates. *The Challenges of Retrenchment.* San Francisco: Jossey-Bass, 1981.

Mitroff, Ian I. *The Subjective Side of Science.* Amsterdam: Elsevier, 1974.

Nunnally, J.D. *Psychometric Theory.* New York:
McGraw-Hill, 1978.

Seelmeyer, John. "The Anatomy of a Library School Shutdown." *American Libraries* 16(2):95-96, 113
(February 1985).

Stefonek, Tom. *Cutback Management in Public Organiza-
tions.* Madison: Wisconsin Department of Public
Instruction Division for Management, Planning, and
Federal Services, 1979.

Stueart, Robert D. "Great Expectations: Library and Information Science Education at the Crossroads."
Library Journal 106(18):1989-1992.

Weathersby, George B. "Scarce Resources Can Be a Golden
Opportunity for Higher Education." *Change*
14(2):12-13 (March 1982).

West, T.W. "The Right Way to Close." *AGB Reports* 37-44
(August 1980).

White, Herbert S. "Accreditation and the Pursuit of Excellence." *Journal of Education for Librarianship*
23(4):253-263 (Spring 1983).

White, Herbert S. "Critical Mass for Library Education."
American Libraries 10(8):468-470, 479-481.

Winkler, Karen J. "Questioning the Science in Social
Science, Scholars Signal a 'Turn to Interpretation.'"
The Chronicle of Higher Education 30(17):5-6 (June
26, 1985).

Willmer, W.K. and O'Connor, M.J. "Closing with Compassion." *AGB Reports* 27-31 (November/De-
cember, 1979).

Yin, Robert K. *Case Study Research: Design and Methods*. Beverly Hills: Sage Publications, 1984.

Yin, Robert K. "The Case Study as a Serious Research Methodology." *Knowledge: Creation, Diffusion, Utilization* 3(1):97–114 (September, 1981).

INDEX